BOOK 3

A STUDENT'S GUIDE AND WORKBOOK
ENGLISH GRAMMAR

John Lee

STONE TOWER PRESS

A Student's Guide and
Workbook to English Grammar
Book 3

Stone Tower Press
7 Ellen Rd.
Middletown, RI 02842
stonetowerpress.com

Paperback ISBN: 978-1-7368651-5-6

Formatting and cover design by Amy Cole, JPL Design Solutions

About the Cover Image:
The classical owl tetradrachm is the most recognized coin of the ancient world. In Greek mythology the owl accompanied Athena, the goddess of wisdom. The owl, in time, became a symbol of knowledge, wisdom, and learning—a veritable mascot of education.

Printed in the United States of America

TABLE OF CONTENTS

TO STUDENTS

This volume completes a "trilogy." It builds upon Books 1 and 2 and adds sections on punctuation, subject/verb agreement, and parallel construction. It also addresses misused words, hypercorrections, and other common mistakes. Like the other volumes, Book 3 starts with review and a diagnostic test. In addition, the material that has been covered in Books 1 and 2 are added as a reference. It is hoped that students come back to this book to refresh their memories.

Because this book deals mostly with common mistakes, I have added copious exercises. However, before rushing to do the exercises, students should work through the examples carefully to make sure that they understand the concepts and pitfalls.

Now for a word of candor. Because students have covered the basics of grammar in Books 1 and 2, they will begin bumping against stylistic considerations. For example, some authors like the Oxford comma, others do not. Some authors place a comma after each prepositional phrase, others only after prepositional phrases that are longer than five words. Still others favor flexibility based on the feel and rhythm of the sentence. All of this is to say that there is flexibility. Stylistic considerations add an extra depth of enjoyment to the craft of writing. In time, students will develop their own voices and style. Toward the end of this book, students will see and feel this flexibility. That said, I have taken a more prescriptive approach to language without being draconian, at least that is my intention.

As always, students should not hesitate to ask their teachers questions. Learning the material in class is one of the keys to learning. I also have tried to include works of literature that provoke thinking and discussion. If conversations emerge in class, it is a boon.

Thank you for staying with this series to the end. My hope is that it will offer a strong foundation for the enjoyment of reading, writing, and speaking. Few things in life are as enjoyable as a life of the mind with words.

ACKNOWLEDGMENTS

I'd like to thank my teachers over the years who have sparked in me a love for writing. While I was a graduate student at Yale University, two teachers offered comments on my writing. John Matthews encouraged me to develop a lean style of writing. Jean-Christophe Agnew saw my love for religious texts and encouraged me to develop a poetic vision for my prose. They probably do not remember giving these pieces of advice, but I was listening and took them to heart. I also thank Susie Case, a colleague and now a friend. She helped me with her sage comments. She is an extraordinary guide. I also thank two old friends who encouraged me to put my words on paper long ago, Ashish Raichur and Bryan Lee. They planted the seeds of desire. Finally, I thank my wife, Mimi, who read my writing for years. Without teachers and friends, life would be much more difficult and far less enjoyable. I am thankful for them.

DIAGNOSTIC TEST

I. Identify the underlined words.

"I heard exactly the same thing, a long time ago to be sure, **from a doctor**," the elder remarked. "He was then an old **man**, and unquestionably intelligent. He spoke just as frankly as you, humorously, but with a sorrowful humor. 'I love mankind,' he said, 'but I am amazed at **myself**: the more I love mankind in general, the less I love people in particular, that is, individually, as separate persons. In my dreams,' he said, 'I often went so far as to think passionately of **serving** mankind, and, it may be, would really have gone to the cross for people **if it were somehow suddenly necessary**, and yet I am incapable of living in the same room with anyone even for two days, this I know from experience. **As soon as someone is there**, close to me, his personality oppresses my self-esteem and restricts my freedom. In twenty-four hours, I can begin to hate even the best of men: one because he takes **too** long eating his dinner, another because he has a cold and keeps blowing his nose. I become the enemy of people the moment **they touch me**,' he said. 'On the other hand, it has always happened that the more I hate people individually, the more ardent becomes my love for humanity as a whole.'"

"But what is to be done, then? What is to be done in such a case? Should one fall into despair?"

"No, for it is enough **that you are distressed by it**. Do **what you can**, and it will be reckoned unto you. You have already done much if you can understand yourself so deeply and so sincerely! But if you spoke with me so sincerely just now in order **to be praised**, as I have praised you, for your truthfulness, then of course you will get nowhere with your efforts at active love; it will all remain merely a **dream**, and your whole life will flit by like a phantom. Then, naturally, you will forget about the future life, and in the end will somehow calm down by yourself."

"You have crushed me! Only now, this very moment, as you were speaking, did I realize **that indeed I was waiting only for you to praise my sincerity**, when I told you that I couldn't bear ingratitude. You've brought me back to myself, you've caught me out and explained **me** to myself!"

Fyodor Dostoevsky, *The Brothers Karamazov*

Why is sincerity important for the elder in his dialogue?

II. State how many clauses are in in each sentence and identify the type of sentence. Draw parenthesis around subordinate clauses.

1. "When I have a little money, I buy books; and if I have any left, I buy food and clothes." Erasmus

____

____

2. "The Nellie, a cruising yawl, swung to her anchor without a flutter of the sails, and was at rest." Joseph Conrad, *Heart of Darkness*

3. "I was read to as a small child, I read on my own as soon as I could, and I recall being more or less overwhelmed again and again — not by what books actually said, but by what they suggested, what they helped me to imagine." Marilynne Robinson

4. "'Mind,' he began again, lifting one arm from the elbow, the palm of the hand outwards, so that, with his legs folded before him, he had the pose of a Buddha preaching in European clothes and without a lotus-flower." Joseph Conrad, *Heart of Darkness*

III. Underline all verbals and label them.

1. "Thus spoke Zarathustra and left his cave, glowing and strong, like a morning sun coming out of dark mountains." Friedrich Nietzsche, *Thus Spoke Zarathustra*

2. "With a sudden squawking and flapping of stunted wings all but one rose and dashed helter-skelter, their long legs rising high off the ground as they ran towards open territory." Bryce Courtenay, *The Power of One*

3. "On the morning of January 22, 1998, snow sifted gently over the village once known as Naoetsu. Louis Zamperini, four days short of his eighty-first birthday, stood in a swirl of white beside a road flanked in bright drifts. His body was worn and weathered, his skin scratched with lines mapping the miles of his life. His old riot of black hair was now a translucent scrim of white, but his blue eyes still threw sparks." Laura Hillenbrand, *Unbroken: A World War II Story of Survival, Resilience, and Redemption*

ONE

PARTS OF SPEECH

1. VERBS

1.1 The heart of a sentence is the verb. There are two types of verbs: action and linking.

- Action verbs perform an action.
- Linking verbs do not perform an action. Instead, they connect the subject to what comes after the verb. Think of a linking verb as showing what someone or something is. Examples will make this point clear.

1.2 Action verbs:

- The boy **jumped** over the fence.
- I **hit** the ball.
- **Sit** down!
- Martin **scored** three points in the final seconds.

1.3 Linking verbs:

- My mother **is** a doctor.
- The teacher **will be** pleased.
- The cookies **are** good.
- She **became** a lawyer.
- He **will become** a great writer.
- We **were** friends.

Notice the linking verb shows what someone or something is.

1.4 Apart from the verbs "to be" and "become," there are other linking verbs. Additional linking verbs include *look, prove, smell, sound, taste, appear,* and *feel.*

- To test whether a verb is a linking verb, replace the word with the appropriate form of the verb "to be." If the sentence makes sense, then the verb is a linking verb.
- The cake smells good. = The cake is good.
- She looks elated. = She is elated.
- That pasta tastes amazing. = That pasta is amazing.
- My mother appears satisfied. = My mother is satisfied.
- My friend smelled the roses. ≠ My friend is the roses.
- I looked at the dog. ≠ I am at the dog.
- John tasted the pasta. ≠ John is the pasta.
- My mother felt the kitten. ≠ My mother is the kitten.

1.5 Verbs can include more than one word. When this happens, all the words constitute a verb phrase. The words in the phrase are called helping or auxiliary verbs.

- I **am enjoying** the ice cream.
- I **should be enjoying** the ice cream.
- **Will** I **enjoy** the ice cream? (Notice the verb phrase is broken up by the subject.)
- I **will have been** president by then.
- I **had had** some of the cake. (Don't be fooled by the verb "had" and the auxiliary word "had.")
- She **might be coming** to the party.
- Recognizing verb phrases will help tremendously in Latin composition.
- The farmer is laboring. ~~*Agricola est laborat*~~. *Agricola laborat.*

1.6 Verbs are either passive or active in voice.

- The soldiers defended the city. (Active, the subject does the action.)
- The city was defended by the soldiers. (Passive, the subject receives the action.)
- The girl walked the dog. (Active)
- The dog was walked by the girl. (Passive)

1.7 Negative adverbs are not a part of the verb phrase.

- I **am** not your father, Luke. (Notice that the word, "not" is not in bold.)
- **Will** I not **give** you money? (Helping verbs do not need to be next to the main verb.)
- I **would**n't do that if I **were** you.
- Why **should** I not **spend** my money?

1.8 Action verbs can be either transitive or intransitive.

- Transitive verbs take direct objects and intransitive verbs do not.
- Some verbs are both transitive and intransitive. Context determines the nature of the verb.
- She **bumped** the boy. (Transitive)
- She **hit** the ball with the bat. (Transitive)
- She **walks** in the park. (Intransitive)
- She **walks** the dog in the park. (Transitive)
- She **stands**. (Intransitive)
- She **stands** the book on the table. (Transitive)

1.9 Verbs have three principal parts: Present tense, past tense, and past participle.

- Regular verbs follow a recognizable pattern; irregular verbs must be memorized. With these principal parts, you can create all tenses.
- turn, turned, turned
- yell, yelled, yelled
- sing, sang, sung

2. NOUNS

2.1 There are two types of nouns: abstract and concrete.

- Abstract nouns are not tangible. Your senses cannot detect them. For example, you cannot hold courage or honesty in your hands.
- Concrete nouns are people, places, or things.

2.2 Abstract Nouns:

- The **thoughts** of the great philosopher challenged our **assumptions**.
- The **bravery** of King Leonidas struck **fear** into the hearts of his enemies.
- Solon restructured the Athenian constitution with **skill**.
- I have **reservations** about that.
- My **misery** is only matched by my **poverty**.
- **Honor** comes to the man who displays **integrity**.

2.3 Concrete Nouns:

- He threw the **ball**.
- **Hugo** scored.
- **Penguins** cannot fly, but they waddle well.
- My **mother** cooked the **fish** with the perfect amount of **garlic**, **salt**, and **pepper**.
- I love **books**.
- I dwell in that **building**.

2.4 Nouns can be viewed as either common or proper.

- Common nouns are just as they sound: house, building, pizza, man, air, and paper.
- Proper nouns are specific, usually one-of-a-kind. They are capitalized.
- Dates are also proper nouns.
- Examples: John, King George, 1903, English, Mr. T., New York, World War II.

2.5 Formation of plurals can be tricky.

- Most nouns form their plural by adding s. Desks, tables, and trees.
- If the noun ends in s, sh, x, z, then add “es” to the ending. Gases, taxes, crocuses, and waltzes.

3. ADJECTIVES

3.1 Adjectives modify nouns. They are describing words, which include possessives, articles, demonstratives, indefinites, and numbers.

- **Big** boats sail away into **the** sunset.
- **A black** sea of terror has overwhelmed him. Sophocles, *Oedipus*
- "She is **a** perfectly **terrible** person," said Lucy. C. S. Lewis, *The Lion, The Witch and the Wardrobe*
- **The** ants were **busy** on **the** ground, **big black** ones with **shiny** bodies and **the little dusty quick** ants. John Steinbeck, *The Pearl*

3.2 Possessives:

- **Oedipus's** fault was **his** hubris. (All possessives are adjectives. Whose fault? Oedipus's fault.)
- **His** sight was nothing compared to **Tiresias's** preternatural sight.
- **My** friend lost **his** pen.
- **Our** predicament is not a good one.

Some classify possessives as nouns (genitive case), but in this book we will consider them adjectives.

3.3 Articles:

- "Who controls **the** past controls **the** future. Who controls **the** present controls **the** past." George Orwell, *1984*

- Experience is **the** best teacher.
- **The** teacher got into his red Ferrari and revved **the** engine.
- "I am constant as **the** Northern Star." (Northern Star is a noun.) Shakespeare, *Julius Caesar*
- **An** apple **a** day keeps you healthy.

3.4 Demonstrative adjectives modify nouns. The most common ones are this, these, that, and those.

- **That** man over there is my father. ("There" is an adverb)
- If I hear **those** noises again at midnight, I will run.
- **These** men will go; **those** men will stay.
- Please hand **that** book to me and hand **this** book to Ms. Brooks.

Some classify demonstratives as determiners, but in this book we will consider them adjectives.

3.5 Indefinite adjectives do not refer to any specific person or thing. Hence, they are indefinite. Typical indefinite pronouns are all, any, each, few, many, none, and some.

- **Many** men will try, but only a **few** men will make it.
- He ate **several** pancakes.
- "**All** animals are equal, but **some** animals are more equal than others." George Orwell, *Animal Farm*
- Cowards die **many** times before their actual death.

3.6 Numbers can be considered special adjectives.

- He sentenced **ten** men to jail.
- In **four** hours, we will be in London.

- **"Four** legs good, **two** legs bad." George Orwell, *Animal Farm*
- Numbers always occur before adjectives in a string of words.
- Seven big cats roamed the streets of the city. You cannot say: "Big seven cats…"

3.7 Interrogative adjectives, like other adjectives, modify nouns but they introduce a question.

In Latin: *qui, quae, quod* = interrogative adjectives. These words are not to be confused with relative pronouns, which share the same forms.

- **What** man will stand for justice?
- **Which** car is the fastest?
- **Whose** father is a consul? This could be written as: The father of whom is a consul?
- **Which** opportunity should I take?

3.8 Some adjectives are irregular in the comparative and superlative. Here are the most common irregular adjectives.

Positive	Comparative	Superlative
Bad	Worse	Worst
Many	More	Most
Well	Better	Best
Little	Less	Least

4. PRONOUNS

4.1 Pronouns take the place of nouns.

- Elijah is an actor. **He** is excellent.
- My mother is a great cook. **She** makes the most amazing peach pie.
- Oranges are delicious. **I** crave **them** all the time.
- John and Joan went to the store. **They** bought candy, chips, and soda.
- Jenny and Michelle should go to the movies. **They** would have a great time.
- Mike and **I** love Shake Shack. **We** are going right after school.

4.2 The antecedent refers to the noun that the pronoun replaces. Since the pronoun replaces the noun, the pronoun must match the noun in number and gender.

- Jim and Jamil went to the movies. **They** (Jim and Jamil) left twenty minutes ago.
- The king bequeathed the land to the Romans. **He** (the king) fulfilled his promise.
- Ms. Smith gave us detention. **She** (Ms. Smith) also yelled at us.
- The cashier gave me the wrong change. **He** (cashier) gave me ten extra dollars.
- I hit the ball into the outfield. **It** (the ball) hit my brother in the head.

4.3 Pronouns:

Subject

	Singular	Plural
1st	I	We
2nd	You	You
3rd	He, She, It	They

Object

	Singular	Plural
1st	Me	Us
2nd	You	You
3rd	Him, Her, It	Them

Reflexive

	Singular	Plural
1st	Myself	Ourselves
2nd	Yourself	Yourselves
3rd	Himself, Herself, Itself	Themselves

4.4 Apart from functioning as subjects, pronouns can be objects and predicate nominatives.

- Rachel gave the book to **him**. (Object of preposition)
- Please hand **him** the keys. (Indirect object)
- Here is the pencil. I'll give **it** to you. (Direct object)
- This is **he**. (Predicate nominative)

4.5 Possessive pronouns. Consider possessive pronouns as adjectives.

- I have **his** book. (His is an adjective because it describes what kind of book—his book.)
- **My** cat licked **your** hand. (Whose cat? My cat. Whose hand? Your hand.)
- **Our** friends love playing cards. (Whose friends? Our friends)
- Who took **my** pencil and **his** Latin book? (Don't be thrown off by questions.)

4.6 Interrogative pronouns ask questions. They are: Who? Whose? Whom? Which? What?

If the question word (Which?) comes before the noun, it becomes an interrogative adjective. If it comes after, it becomes a relative clause/adjective clause.

- **Who** ran for president? Interrogative pronoun.
- **What** did he say? Interrogative pronoun.
- **Which** person ran for president? Interrogative adjective.
- **What** disaster struck the city? Interrogative adjective.
- **Whom** did you see at that party? Interrogative pronoun.
- The book **that** is on the table belongs to my mother. Notice "that" introduces a relative clause/adjective clause.

5. ADVERBS

5.1 Adverbs modify verbs, adjectives, and other adverbs.

- The dog **sadly** whimpered. ("Sadly" modifies "whimpered")
- The rent is **too** high. ("Too" modifies high)
- The ninja **very quickly** leapt. ("Very" modifies "quickly," "quickly" modifies "leapt.")
- **Now** is the time to go. ("Now" modifies "is.")
- "I **never** forget a face," my teacher said. ("Never" modifies "forget.")

5.2 Adverbs usually address: when, where, how, and to what degree.

- She ate dinner **early**. (when)
- Lionel Messi kicked the ball **up**. (where)
- The girl studied **diligently**. (how)
- I saw him **yesterday**. (when)
- I'll go **there** with you. (where)
- Stand **up**. (where)
- She was **very** angry. (degree)

5.3 Many adverbs end in "-ly," but not all words that end in "-ly" are adverbs.

- Costly sacrifice—costly is an adjective.
- Deadly force—deadly is an adjective.
- Here are some others: disorderly, ghastly, chilly, bodily, stately, ugly, silly, wily.

- It is worth mentioning that some nouns and verbs also end in "-ly," such as: homily, belly, and supply.

5.4 There are many adverbs that do not have the "-ly" ending.

- Next, forward, not, never, often, always.

5.5 Adverbs also have comparative and superlative forms.

- I watch movies **more frequently** than my brother.
- His dog attacks **most fiercely** when he is hungry.

5.6 The position of the adverb is flexible, but it should be close to the word it modifies.

- Carefully he opened the package.
- He carefully opened the package.

5.7 Conjunctive Adverbs. We will revisit conjunctive adverbs when we cover clauses.

- Some common conjunctive adverbs: accordingly, also, besides, finally, furthermore, hence, however, indeed, instead, meanwhile, moreover, rather, similarly, then, therefore, thus, and yet.

5.8 Use adverbs sparingly. Strong verbs make for vigorous prose. The words of Stephen King are apropos.

"...[Adverbs are] like dandelions. If you have one on your lawn, it looks pretty unique. If you fail to root it out, however, you find five the next day...fifty the day after that...and then, my brothers and sisters, your lawn is totally, completely, and profligately covered with dandelions. By then you see them for the weeds they really are, but they then it's – GASP!! – too late."

5.9 Some words can be both adverbs and adjectives. Context is key. Ask what word is modified.

- That is a fast car.
- He was driving too fast.
- The early train leaves at noon.
- The train arrive three minutes early.
- That is a hard surface.
- Don't work too hard.

6. PREPOSITIONS

6.1 Prepositional phrases show a relationship within a sentence between the object of the preposition and other words in the sentence.

6.2 Common Prepositions:

About	Below	In	Out
Above	Besides	In front of	Outside
Across	Between	Inside	Over
After	Beyond	In spite of	Regarding
Against	By	Instead of	Since
Along	Concerning	Into	Through
Among	Despite	Like	Throughout
Around	Down	Near	To
At	During	Of	Towards
Because of	Except	On	Under
Before	For	Onto	Up
Behind	From	Out	With / Within / Without

6.3 Prepositions cannot stand by themselves. Prepositions have objects, which are nouns or pronouns.

- Above the table
- Behind the building
- Since the game
- Towards the beach

- Instead of him
- From them

6.4 Choose a word such as "house" as the object of the preposition to determine whether a word is a preposition. This approach will help in most cases.

- About the house, across the house, after the house, against the house, along the house, among the houses, besides the house, by the house, down the house, except the house, regarding the house, etc.

6.5 Certain prepositions can be adverbs or subordinate conjunctions. If there is no *object*, it is an adverb or a subordinate conjunction.

- I stood **up** on the table. ("Up" is an adverb.)
- I wore **out** my pants. ("Out" is an adverb.)
- I looked **up**. ("Up" is an adverb.)
- **Before** I run in the mornings, I eat breakfast. ("Before" is a subordinate conjunction.)

6.6 Some argue that prepositions can take clauses, but in this book, we will make a distinction between subordinate conjunctions and prepositions. The former creates a clause, the latter a phrase.

6.7 A note on style:

Get rid of unnecessary prepositions.

- The boy met **up with** the new students. = The boy met the new students.

- Where are you **at**? = Where are you?
- It is inside **of** the house. = It is inside the house.

6.8 There are several idiomatic expressions that you need to memorize. In time you will get a sense of these expressions.

- I live on 57th street; I live in an apartment; I live with my family; I live at the end of the road.
- I argue about an issue, I argue with a person; I argue against the law.

7. CONJUNCTIONS

7.1 There are two types of conjunctions.

- Coordinating conjunctions join words, phrases, or clauses.
- Subordinating conjunctions join dependent or subordinate clauses to an independent clause.

7.2 Coordinating conjunctions:

The most common coordinating conjunctions follow the acronym: F-A-N-B-O-Y-S. For, And, Nor, But, Or, Yet, and So.

- He did not want to waste money, **for** he learned the value of making a dollar.
- Caesar was generous **and** merciful.
- I do not like to eat after six, **nor** do I like to drink after ten.
- Brutus loved Casear, **but** he loved Rome more.
- You may have milk **or** orange juice, not both.
- I won the lottery, **yet** I am not happy.
- General Patton believed in leading by doing, **so** he fought in the fray with his men.

7.3 A note on style:

Even though some shun starting a sentence with "but" and "and," it is within the bounds of proper grammar to start a sentence with either conjunction.

- The hawks won the day, as everyone in the senate voted in favor of war. But one voice dissented.

7.4 This list contains the most common subordinate conjunctions.

After	Although	As	As if
As long as	As though	Because	Before
Even if	Even though	If	If only
In order that	Rather than	Since	So that
Than	That	Though	Unless
When	Whenever	Where	Whereas
While			

Subordinate conjunctions create subordinate clauses.

- **After I ran the marathon**, I needed rest.
- **Even though I ran the marathon**, I feel fine.
- **Because I left New York**, I miss pizza and bagels.

7.5 Omission of "that." The word "that" may be omitted.

- Artemis knew that Luke would call him after dinner.
- Artemis knew Luke would call him after dinner.
- Luke thought **that** Artemis might be busy.
- Luke thought Artemis might be busy.

Notice that the word "that" is optional.

8. INTERJECTIONS

8.1 Interjections show feelings and bursts of emotions.

- Whoa! That was close.
- Oops, I did it again!
- Zoinks, Scooby!
- Eureka! I found the answer.
- Shhh!
- tut tut
- tsk tsk
- Oh!
- Ouch!
- Gosh!
- Yikes!

8.2 Be careful that you do not confuse imperatives and interjections. Imperatives are verbs.

- Sit down!
- Close the door!

8.3 Interjections can take different punctuation marks. With a little practice, you will get the hang of interjections without problems.

- Huh? What did you mean by that?
- Pssst, pass the sugar.

PARTS OF SPEECH TEST:

I. Underline the nouns.

CURSED, cursed creator! Why did I live? Why, in that instant, did I not extinguish the spark of existence which you had so wantonly bestowed?

II. Underline the verbs.

I know not; despair had not yet taken possession of me; my feelings were those of rage and revenge. I could with pleasure have destroyed the cottage and its inhabitants and have glutted myself with their shrieks and misery.

III. Underline the adjectives (include articles).

When night came, I quitted my retreat, and wandered in the wood; and now, no longer restrained by the fear of discovery, I gave vent to my anguish in fearful howlings. I was like a wild beast that had broken the toils; destroying the objects that obstructed me and ranging through the wood with a stag-like swiftness.

IV. Underline the adverbs.

Oh! what a miserable night I passed! the cold stars shone in mockery, and the bare trees waved their branches above me: now and then the sweet voice of a bird burst forth amidst the universal stillness. All, save I, were at rest or in enjoyment: I, like the arch fiend, bore a hell within me; and, finding myself unsympathized with, wished to tear up the trees, spread havoc and destruction around me, and then to have sat down and enjoyed the ruin.

V. Underline the prepositional phrases.

But this was a luxury of sensation that could not endure; I became fatigued with excess of bodily exertion and sank on the damp grass in the sick impotence of despair.

VI. Underline the conjunctions and circle the pronouns.

"There was none among the myriads of men that existed who would pity or assist me; and should I feel kindness towards my enemies? No: from that moment I declared everlasting war against the species, and, more than all, against him who had formed me, and sent me forth to this insupportable misery. The sun rose; I heard the voices of men and knew that it was impossible to return to my retreat during that day. Accordingly, I hid myself in some thick underwood, determining to devote the ensuing hours to reflection on my situation."

Mary Shelley, F*rankenstein*

TWO

PARTS OF THE SENTENCE

9. THE PREDICATE

9.1 All sentences must have at least one predicate. The predicate tells what the subject is doing. The verb (action or linking) is the essential part of the predicate. See §1.1-1.9.

9.2 Action:

- I **ran** the marathon.
- Oliver and Walker **won** the game with their teamwork.
- **Stop**!
- They **danced** the night away.
- She **leapt** over the wall.

9.3 Linking:

- We **are** farmers.
- They **are** good sailors.
- She **became** a doctor.
- I **will be** a grammarian.
- The flowers **smell** good.

9.4 Verb phrases contain helping verbs.

- They **will have bought** the present.
- **Would** they **have finished** the assignment?
- The boys **were running** down the hallway.
- **Should** I **run** for office? (Helping verbs can be separated from the main verb.)

9.5 Compound verbs:

- They **will run** and **walk**.
- **Watch** and **learn**.

9.6 Verbs are either passive or active in voice.

- In the active voice, the subject performs the action.
- In the passive voice, the subject receives the action.
- The little girl **ate** the cupcake. Active. The subject performs the action.
- The cupcake **was eaten** by the little girl. The subject receives the action; the cupcake (subject) was eaten.
- The burglar **broke** the door. Active.
- The door **was broken** by the burglar. Passive.

Make these sentences passive:

1. The batter hit the ball out of the park.
2. He whipped the cream to perfection.
3. Bravery won the day.
4. More than other kings, Sargon focused his attention on expansion.
5. The man carried the box of books up the winding stairs.

10. THE SUBJECT

10.1 The best way to find the subject is first to look for the verb of the sentence. Ask who or what is doing the action of the verb.

- **Oedipus** solved the riddle of the sphinx.
- My **brother** loved the novel.
- **Charlie** won the golden ticket.
- **I** pleased my mother with good grades.
- **Christmas** came early this year.
- **He** jumped over the fence, the gate, and the wall.

10.2 If the verb is passive, then the subject receives the action. The thing or person doing the action is usually followed by the preposition "by."

- The **man** was hit by the ball.
- The winning **ticket** was bought by the man.
- The **men** were seen by the enemies.

10.3 Some sentences are imperatival. In these cases, there is an implied "you" as the subject.

- Be quiet in the auditorium. (The subject is an implied "you.")
- In the stillness of morning, don't spoil the tranquility. (Don't let the prepositional phrase confuse you. The subject is still an implied "you.")
- Bring the wood from the forest. We need to start a fire.
- Stop it!
- Please pass the sugar.

10.4 When you have a linking verb, the subject is not actually *performing the action of the verb*. Examples will make this point clear.

- **He** is a good boy.
- **Christian** was in school.
- **Creon** and **Jocasta** were in Thebes.
- **He** will be the president of the company.
- The **roses** smell good. (The roses are not sniffing, right?)

10.5 Compound subjects:

- **Snowball** and **Napoleon** were joint leaders of Animal Farm.
- **Atticus** and **Scout** sat under the tree and talked about life.
- **Ozymandias** and **Colossus** had delusions of grandeur.
- **John**, **Max**, **Shelly**, **Ryan**, and **Addie** all came to my place.
- **Rain** and **hail** destroyed our manicured lawn.
- **Strength** and **honor** propelled the legionaries towards audacity.

10.6 Interrogatives. Don't let the question mark at the end of the sentence confuse you. Rewrite the sentence into a declarative, and you will quickly locate the subject.

- Did **E.T.** really phone home? If you make this sentence into a declarative, it will read: "E.T. really did phone home." At this point, the subject is clear.
- How was **Michael Jordan** able to make that incredible shot?
- Do **you** know Babe Ruth's record?

- Did you know that Babe Ruth was married at St. Gregory's Church on W 90th street?
- Will **he** arrive on time to catch the show?
- Was the **speech** of the queen inspiring?

10.7 Finally, don't let word order fool you. The verb or other parts of speech can come before the noun. Rewriting the sentence can help in these situations.

- On top of the tower beautifully chimed the bells. (The bells on top of the tower chimed beautifully.)
- Hurriedly through the dense forest ran **Robin** towards safety.
- During the plague in Athens **depression** descended.
- Over sea, land, and air ours will be the **victory**.
- Yours are the **trophies**; ours the **glory**. (What is the verb of the second part of the sentence?)

10.8 Appositives always agree in case with the word with which it is in apposition.

- The judge sentenced us—my two friends, my brother, and me.
- My son, Luke, is a lawyer.
- My son, the lawyer, lives in Boston.

10.9 The predicate nominative is not the subject but says something about the subject. It follows a linking verb.

- My friend is a **doctor**.
- She became an **actress**.

11. DIRECT OBJECTS

11.1 Direct objects are nouns or pronouns (even clauses) that receive the action of the verb. To locate the direct object, find the verb and ask, "*verb* what or *verb* whom."

- She hit the **ball**. (Hit what? Hit whom? Ball.)
- The boys threw the **can**. (Threw what? Can.)
- Michael crashed the **car**. (Crashed what? Car.)
- Jack played the **drums**. (Played what? Drums.)
- Help **me**! (Help whom? Me.)
- The boys bought **what they wanted**. (Bought what? What they wanted. We will cover noun clauses in §16.)

11.2 In Latin the accusative case is the direct object.

- *Agricolae frumentum portant.* The farmers carry the grain.
- *Nautae viros malos vulneraverunt.* The sailors have wounded the bad men.

11.3 Not all sentences contain a direct object.

- She runs in the park. (Runs what? Runs whom? Nothing makes sense. "Park" is the object of the preposition.)
- The fish swam into the glass of the tank. (Swam what? Swam whom? Nothing makes sense. "Glass" is the object of the preposition.)
- Marcus is a soldier in Caesar's tenth legion. (Tricky. Soldier is a predicate nominative. Predicate nominatives are not direct objects. See §10.9, §16.8.)

11.4 Action verbs are either transitive or intransitive. Transitive verbs can take a direct object and intransitive verbs cannot. Some verbs are both transitive and intransitive. Context is key.

- The dog bumped the boy. (Transitive. Boy = direct object.)
- The boy threw a ball. (Transitive. Ball = direct object.)
- She walks in the garden. (Intransitive. Park = object of preposition.)
- He walks the dog in the park. (Transitive. Dog = direct object.)
- She stands on the mountain. (Intransitive. No direct object. Mountain = object of the preposition.)
- She stands the book on the table. (Transitive. Book = direct object.)

11.5 General Formula. Subject + Verb + What? / Whom? = Direct Object.

- This formula works not only with nouns and pronouns but also clauses. See §16 for a discussion on noun clauses.
- Achilles threw the **javelin,** and it hit the **man** on the horse.
- Dr. Seuss wrote my favorite **books**.
- She gave **what she wanted to give**. ("What she wanted to give" is a noun clause.)
- She hopes **that he will come home**. ("That he will come home" is a noun clause.)

12. INDIRECT OBJECTS

12.1 An indirect object tells to or for whom or what the action of the verb has been done. The indirect object comes before the direct object. To find the indirect object, ask ***to or for whom***. Examples will make this point clear.

- The teacher gave **me** the answer. (Gave what? The answer. To whom? Me)
- The magnanimous donor gave the **school** a check for a hundred million dollars. (Gave what? A check. To whom or what? The school)
- The father threw **me** the ball. (Threw what? The ball. To whom? Me)
- I told **you** the truth. (Told what? The truth. To whom? You)
- The painter showed the **audience** his magnum opus. (Showed what? His magnum opus. To whom? the audience)

12.2 In Latin the case of the indirect object is the dative.

- *Donum tibi dedi.* I gave you the gift.

12.3 Indirect objects can be made into prepositional phrases. Latin students, proceed with caution. In English, prepositional phrases are not indirect objects though they can replace the indirect object.

- The teacher gave the answer **to me**.
- The magnanimous donor gave a check for a hundred million dollars **to the school**.

- The father threw the ball **to me**.
- I told the truth **to you**.
- The painter showed his magnum opus **to the audience**.

12.4 Indirect objects are moderately rare. In order to have an indirect object, you need a transitive verb and a direct object. Without both, you cannot have an indirect object.

12.5 Common verbs that have indirect objects.

- Buy, get, cook, keep, bring, give, lend, offer, pass, send, show, and promise.

13. PREPOSITIONAL PHRASES

13.1 Common Prepositions:

About	Below	In	Out
Above	Besides	In front of	Outside
Across	Between	Inside	Over
After	Beyond	In spite of	Regarding
Against	By	Instead of	Since
Along	Concerning	Into	Through
Among	Despite	Like	Throughout
Around	Down	Near	To
At	During	Of	Towards
Because of	Except	On	Under
Before	For	Onto	Up
Behind	From	Out	With / Within / Without

13.2 Prepositions cannot stand by themselves. Prepositions have objects, which are nouns or pronouns.

- Behind the garden
- Before the garden
- Under the garden
- Within the garden
- From the garden

13.3 Prepositions are either adjectival or adverbial. If a prepositional phrase is adjectival, it will modify a noun or a pronoun; if it is adverbial, it will modify a verb, adjective, or another adverb.

13.4 Adjectival prepositional phrases:

- Adjectival prepositional phrases usually answer the question "which one."
- Another trick: if you can make the prepositional phrase into a relative clause, you are dealing with an adjectival prepositional phrase.
- The cup **on the stand** contains milk. (The cup, which is on the stand, contains milk. Which cup? The one on the stand.)
- The wolves **of the forest** howl. (The wolves, which are of the forest, howl. Which wolves? The ones in the forest.)
- The delegates **from New England** were pleasant. (The delegates, who are from New England, were pleasant. Which delegates? The ones from New England.)
- The strawberries **in my mother's** garden are the best I've ever eaten. (The strawberries, which are in my mother's garden, are the best I've ever eaten. Which strawberries? The ones in my mother's garden.)

13.5 Adverbial prepositional phrases:

- Adverbial prepositional phrases usually answer the question of **how, when, or where.**
- She ran **into the bathroom** because she had a bloody nose. (Where? "Into the bathroom" modifies "ran.")

- The mouse scurried **underneath the train tracks** never to be seen again. (Where? "Underneath the train tracks" modifies "scurried.")
- **During the play** Jeff yawned. (When? "During the play" modifies "yawn")
- **After dinner** we chatted **for hours**. (When? "After dinner" modifies "chatted.")
- The car sped **with great skill**. (How? "With great skill" modifies "sped.")

14. APPOSITIVES

14.1 Appositives occur when two or more nouns are placed next to each other and refer to the same thing. What comes after the first noun is in apposition. It gives further information. Examples will make this point clear.

- My son, **a lawyer**, lives in New York.
- On our way to Philadelphia, we stopped by Cherry Hill, **a sleepy suburb in New Jersey**.

14.2 Do no confuse appositives with items in a list.

- In college, I lived in a cramped off-campus apartment with Jeff, John, and Matt.
- Note that Jeff, John, and Matt are in a list.

14.3 Appositives are akin to relative clauses without the relative pronoun and verb.

- The coffee shop, a hole in the wall, serves the best cup of cappuccino.
- The coffee shop, which is a hole in the wall, serves the best cup of cappuccino.

14.4 Appositives often comprise of phrases, not just a single word.

- I saw a rare bird in the park, **a beautiful red-tailed hawk with a field mouse in his claws**.

PARTS OF THE SENTENCE TEST:

I. Draw boxes around the subjects, circle direct objects, and underline prepositional phrases.

"124 WAS SPITEFUL. Full of a baby's venom. The women in the house knew it and so did the children. For years each put up with the spite in his own way, but by 1873 Sethe and her daughter Denver were its only victims. The grandmother, Baby Suggs, was dead, and the sons, Howard and Buglar, had run away by the time they were thirteen years old—as soon as merely looking in a mirror shattered it (that was the signal for Buglar); as soon as two tiny hand prints appeared in the cake (that was it for Howard). Neither boy waited to see more; another kettleful of chickpeas smoking in a heap on the floor; soda crackers crumbled and strewn in a line next to the door sill. Nor did they wait for one of the relief periods: the weeks, months even, when nothing was disturbed. No. Each one fled at once—the moment the house committed what was for him the one insult not to be borne or witnessed a second time. Within two months, in the dead of winter, leaving their grandmother, Baby Suggs; Sethe, their mother; and their little sister, Denver, all by themselves in the gray and white house on Bluestone Road. It didn't have a number then, because Cincinnati didn't stretch that far. In fact, Ohio had been calling itself a state only seventy years when first one brother and then the next stuffed quilt packing into his hat, snatched up his shoes, and crept away from the lively spite the house felt for them."

Toni Morrison, *Beloved*

II. Give the part of the sentence of the underlined words.

"I was the youngest **child** in the school by two years, and I spoke only English, the infected tongue that had spread like a **plague** into the sacred land and contaminated the pure, sweet waters of Afrikanerdom.

The Boer War had created a great **malevolence** for the English, for the Rooineks. It was a hate that had entered their **bloodstream** and pocked the hearts and minds of the next generation. To their barefoot sons, I was the first live example of the congenital hate they carried for my kind.

I spoke the language **which** had pronounced the sentences that had killed their grandfathers and sent their grandmothers to the world's first concentration camps, where they died like flies from dysentery, malaria, and black water fever. To the bitter **Calvinist** farmers, the sins of the fathers had been visited upon the sons, unto the third generation. I was infected.

I had had no previous warning that I was **wicked** and it came as a fearful surprise. I was blubbing to myself in the little kids' dormitory **when** suddenly I was dragged from under my horrid camphor-smelling blanket by two eleven-year-olds and taken to the **seniors'** dormitory, to stand trial before the council of war."

Bryce Courtenay, *The Power of One*

III. Underline and label all objects (direct, indirect, and prepositional).

1. Over the mountain ranges lies the village.
2. The boy shouted, "Give it to me, or I will tell my mother."
3. Shall we send you the documents overnight even if it costs three times the price?
4. That is a difficult issue. You should consult a professional technician concerning networking problems.
5. The critics say that viewers should give the movie a try because the cinematography is amazing.
6. Throwing a fastball at 90 miles an hour is the hallmark of the freshman.
7. The dog sniffed the flowers and then ran into the woods.
8. People may forget what you said and may even forget you, but they will remember how you made them feel.
9. Did Einstein say: "Imagination is everything; it is the preview of life's coming attractions?"
10. "Always forgive your enemies; nothing annoys them so much." Oscar Wilde

THREE

CLAUSES

15. CLAUSES

15.1 A clause has a subject and a verb unlike a phrase which has no subject or verb. Clauses can be independent or dependent/ subordinate.

- When I came home... (Dependent)
- After John and Jane ate dinner... (Dependent)
- The boys ran the race. (Independent)

15.2 An Independent clause is a group of words that contains a subject and a verb and can stand by itself.

- She sang a beautiful song.
- The construction workers razed the building.
- The computer broke.

15.3 A dependent clause is a group of words that contains a subject and verb, but the clause cannot stand alone. It requires an independent clause to complete the sentence.

- Since I ate lunch…
- Whenever I read *To Kill a Mockingbird*…
- Because I finished my project…
- Although I am tired…
- Since I ate lunch, I am not hungry.
- Whenever I read *To Kill a Mockingbird*, I remember 7th grade.
- Because I finished my project, I am going to the movies.
- Although I am tired, I will continue to work.

15.4 There are three types of sentences: simple, compound, and complex. Simple sentences have one independent clause. Compound sentences have at least two independent clauses. Complex sentences have at least one dependent and one independent clause.

- Michael plays the drums. (simple)
- Michael plays the drums, but Gabriel plays the bass. (compound)
- When Michael plays the drums, Gabriel plays the bass. (complex)
- Michael plays the drums, and Gabriel plays the bass whenever they come together. (compound-complex sentence)

15.5 There are three types of subordinate clauses: adjectival, adverbial, and noun clauses. We will only cover the first two for now. Noun clauses will be covered in §16.

15.6 An adjectival clause modifies or describes a noun or pronoun.

- The man, **who is standing there**, is my professor. (Which man? The one over there.)
- James, **whom you saw at the party**, is going to Yale next year to study history. (Which James? The one you saw at the party.)
- Here comes the CEO **by whom the company was restructured**. (Which CEO? The one by whom the company was restructured.)
- This is the book **that I love**. (Which book? The one I love.)
- This is the book **I love**. (Notice that "that" may be omitted.)

Think of the relative clause in Latin.

- *Vidi eos qui ad insulam navigaverunt.* I saw those who sailed to the island.
- *Imperator cui periculum nuntiatum est milites ad castra duxit.* The general to whom the danger was announced led the soldiers to the camp.
- *Qui pecuniam dat bonus amicus est.* He who gives money is a good man.

15.7 Adverbial clauses, like adverbs, modify verbs, adjectives, or adverbs. It is introduced by a subordinate conjunction, such as: if, when, because, until, while, etc.

- **Whenever the markets tumble**, I take a deep breath and take a walk.
- **Because she was late for a month**, the company fired her.
- **After I get ready for bed**, I read a chapter of my favorite author.
- **Since taking my vacation**, I feel like a new woman.
- **If I work diligently**, I will succeed. Keep in mind that conditionals ("if" and "unless") introduce adverbial clauses.
- Adverbial clauses can also come after the main clause. When this happens, no comma is needed. I take a deep breath and take a walk **whenever the markets tumble**.

15.8 Adverbial clauses cannot be the object of a preposition.

- It is like ~~when you fall and get hurt~~.
- It is like falling and getting hurt.

15.9 Adverbial clauses cannot be predicate nominatives.

- The reason I love New York City is ~~because there is so much to see and do~~.
- The reason I love New York City is that there is so much to see and do.

16. NOUN CLAUSES

16.1 A noun clause is a clause (has a subject and verb), but it functions as a noun. Often the noun clause can be replaced with the word, "it."

16.2 Clauses as nouns:

- Taco Bell made me sick. (Taco Bell is clearly the subject.)
- **What I ate** made me sick. (What I ate = noun clause = subject.)
- I love Taco Bell. (Taco Bell is the direct object.)
- I love **what my mother makes**. (What my mother makes = noun clause = direct object.)
- I will give Taco Bell a try. (Taco Bell is the indirect object.)
- I will give whatever you give me a try. (Whatever you give me = noun clause = indirect object.)

Use the substitution method. Replace the noun clause with a noun or pronoun to see if it makes sense.

16.3 Wherever you have a noun, it can be replaced with a noun clause. This means that noun clauses can be subjects, direct objects, indirect objects, objects of a preposition, predicate nominatives, and appositives.

16.4 Subjects:

- **What I made** pleased my family.

- **How we got the piano into that narrow door** boggles my mind.
- **How he gives** inspires me.

16.5 Direct objects:

- I love **whatever he does**.
- I hate **that I love you**.
- Ask **what he wants for his birthday**.

16.6 Indirect objects:

- I will give **whatever my mother asks me** a try.
- Your parents will probably give **what you desire** some thought.
- The judge will give **what the defense said** serious consideration.

16.7 Object of Preposition:

- He never cares about **what the people think**.
- From **where I am standing**, I cannot see the opera.
- Did the conduct committee punish the boys for **how they behaved**?

16.8 Predicate Nominative:

- I am **what I eat**.
- The situation is **that you don't have any money**.
- A computer is **what I wanted for Christmas**.

16.9 Appositive:

- The problem, **that you lost your keys twice**, is bothersome.
- The suggestion, **that you do your work well in advance**, is a good one.
- We stayed in Lancaster, **a pleasant and historic city of moderate size.**

16.10 When a sentence starts with "it" and does not have an antecedent, then "it" is not a subject pronoun. It is a placeholder, and the noun clause is the subject.

Examples will make this point clearer.

- It is sad that I have to repeat myself. = That I have to repeat myself is sad.
- It is true that he did it. = That he did it is true.
- Is it a proven fact that elephants have good memories? That elephants have good memories is a proven fact. (Notice that the interrogative has been made into a declarative sentence).
- It is great that he is coming to the party. = That he is coming to the party is great.
- It was a shock that the Mets won that game in the ninth inning. = That the Mets won that game in the ninth inning was a shock.

17. WHO AND WHOM?

Deciding between who/whom does not have to be difficult. With a little practice, you will master the difference. Read through the following steps and practice.

17.1 Isolate the clause or phrase.

- Once you find the who/whom clause or phrase, ask what the clause or phrase requires.
- If the clause or phrase requires a subject, then "who" is correct.
- If the clause or phrase requires an object, then "whom" is correct.
- To who/whom will she give the book? To = prepositional phrase, which means you need an object. "Whom" is correct.
- Who/whom will manage the company? "Who" is correct because you need a subject.

17.2 Substitution Method:

- The easiest way to determine whether who/whom is correct, substitute he/him or she/her.
- If the sentence is an interrogative, then turn it into a declarative sentence, and then use the substitution method.

EXAMPLES:

- You covered that story about who/whom? = Did you cover that story about he/him? "Him" is obviously the choice.
- For who/whom will she postpone the flight? = She will postpone the flight for he or him. "Him" is the clear choice.

17.3 More Difficult Sentences:

- Predicate Nominative. Try this one: Do you know who/whom I am?
- The answer is actually "who," because the verb "am" is a linking verb that requires a predicate nominative.

17.4 The hardest sentences are those that have a conflict of interest—the who/whom plays a roles in two clauses. In other words, who/whom plays a role in the main clause and the dependent clause. In these cases, the dependent clause wins.

- Try this one. Just hurry up and pass the ball to whoever/whomever is open. Since "to whoever/whomever is open" is the dependent clause, it wins out. "Whoever" is the correct answer.

18. TYPES OF SENTENCES

18.1 There are four types of sentences: simple, compound, complex, and compound complex.

18.2 Simple sentences have one independent clause.

- The car careened off the road.
- The teacher handed out the test.

18.3 Compound sentences have at least two independent clauses.

- The car careened off the road, but the driver avoided the tree.
- The teacher handed out the test, and the students received them.

18.4 Complex sentences have an independent clause and at least one dependent clause.

- Although the car careened off the road, the driver avoided the tree.
- When the teacher handed out the tests, the students were excited.

18.5 Compound complex sentences have at least two independent clause and one dependent clause.

- Although the car careened off the road, the driver avoided the tree, but the cow was not so lucky.

- When the teacher handed out the tests, the students were excited, and they cheered.

CLAUSE TEST

I. How many clauses are in each sentence? Also identify the type of sentence (simple, complex, compound, compound-complex).

1. A carriage house on 80th street has five stories, reaching sixty feet into the ether, and perched on its roof, a garden of Japanese maples and sedum, a miniature oasis of green and fiery red among brick and stone structures.

____

____

2. Each floor houses the work of artists from around the world from cities like Auckland and Tel Aviv to homely hamlets like Princeton and even forbidden capitals like Pyongyang.

____

____

3. Within the Greco-Roman world, honor was the highest currency, and so all sought it.

____

____

4. Almost psychopaths have three main characteristics—lack of empathy, a willingness to engage in immoral behavior, and extreme egocentricity.

____

____

5. They are also superficially charming and glib, which allows them to take advantage of others and go undetected.

____

____

6. She said that what she read last night was the best book that she has ever read.

____

____

7. In the least, this story reveals a long known open secret, that inequalities in the admissions process exist.

____

____

8. C. S. Lewis believes that the modern man is concave, and what is even more alarming is that our educational system is the engine creating this deformity.

____

____

9. "If you want to go fast, go alone; but if you want to go far, go together." An African Proverb

____

____

10. The politician said that we should not focus on what divides us but on what unites us.

____

____

II. Draw parentheses around subordinate clauses and label them—adjectival, adverbial, and nominal, drawing arrows where appropriate.

1. The CEO knew what mattered most for his company—not erudition or eloquence but kindness and compassion.
2. He shows us that no one is infallible because he is honest with his own shortcomings.

3. The anthropologist said that since we all have blind spots, experiencing how others live is an exercise in growing in tolerance and understanding.
4. My point is that we need to learn the material more deeply.
5. That sincerity is precious is obvious, but the question is whether it is prized.
6. It would be helpful to know how the student came to this meaning, but what is more impressive is that he made the right conclusion.
7. According to Paul, the Corinthians were unwilling to lower themselves to accommodate those whom they viewed as social inferiors.
8. These words, coming from the grave, as it were, from a faceless shape, filled me with terror. Elie, Wiesel, *Night*
9. Looking at the shafted sun, Francie had that same fine feeling that came when she recalled the poem they recited in school. Betty Smith, *A Tree Grows in Brooklyn*
10. The rogues sat up the whole of the night before the day on which the procession was to take place, and had sixteen lights burning, so that everyone might see how anxious they were to finish the emperor's new suit. Hans Andersen, "The Emperor's New Clothes"

III. Draw parentheses around dependent clauses and label them.

"I AM a sick man.... I am an angry man. I am an unattractive man. I think there is something wrong with my liver. But I don't understand the least thing about my illness, and I don't know for certain what part of me is affected. I am not having any treatment for it, and never have had, although I have a great respect for medicine and for doctors. I am besides extremely superstitious, if only in having such respect for medicine. (I am well educated enough not to be superstitious, but superstitious I am.) No, I refuse treatment out of spite. That is something you will probably not understand. Well, I understand it. I can't of course explain who my spite is directed against in this matter; I know perfectly well that I can't 'score off' the doctors in any way by not consulting them; I know better than anybody that I am harming nobody but myself. All the same, if I don't have treatment, it is out of spite. Is my liver out of order?—let it get worse!

I have been living like this for a long time now—about twenty years. I am forty. I once used to work in the government service, but I don't now. I was a bad civil servant. I was rude, and I enjoyed being rude. After all, I didn't take bribes, so I had to have some compensation. (A poor witticism; but I won't cross it out. When I wrote it down, I thought it would seem very pointed: now, when I see that I was simply trying to be clever and cynical, I shall leave it in on purpose.) When people used to come to the desk where I sat, asking for information, I snarled at them, and was hugely delighted when I succeeded in hurting somebody's feelings…I was lying when I said just now that I was a bad civil servant. I was lying out of spite. I was simply playing a game with the officer and my other callers; in reality I never could make myself malevolent. I was always conscious of many elements showing the directly opposite tendency. I felt them positively swarming inside me, these elements. I knew they had swarmed there all my life, asking to be let out, but I wouldn't let them out, I wouldn't, I wouldn't."

Fyodor Dostoyevsky, *Notes from the Underground*

FOUR

VERBALS

19. GERUNDS

19.1 Gerunds are verbal nouns. Like verbs they can take adverbial modifiers and objects. But they function as nouns.

19.2 Gerunds end in –ing. However, not all words that end in –ing are gerunds.

- **Studying** is a virtue.
- **Running** a marathon is not easy.
- I gave **playing** the violin my greatest effort.
- My parents have a swimming pool in their backyard. (Note: "swimming" ends in "ing," but it is not a gerund. It is an adjective.)
- The officer gave me a speeding ticket. (Again "speeding" is not a gerund.)
- Nothing interests me. ("Nothing" is a noun.)

19.3 Gerunds can function in all the ways a noun can. This means that they can be subjects, direct objects, indirect objects, objects of prepositions, predicate nominatives, and appositives.

- **Running** is my favorite sport. (Subject)
- I like **eating** good foods. (Direct object)
- The boy gave **studying** Latin his best effort. (Indirect object)
- Without **staying** on course, you will veer off the narrow path. (Object of the preposition)
- Her desire was **winning** at all costs. (Predicate nominative)

- His new job, **testing** game consoles for money, is unbelievable. (Appositive)

19.4 Since gerunds are *verbal* nouns, words can modify gerunds (adverbs and adjectives), and they can take objects.

- **Running a company** takes intelligence, effort, and good luck. ("Company" is the direct object of "running.")
- I enjoy **taking brisk walks** at the crack of dawn. ("Walks" is the direct object of "taking." "Taking" is the direct object of the sentence.)
- **By struggling constantly**, the men have developed character and stamina. ("Constantly" is the adverb that modifies "struggling." "Struggling is the object of the preposition")
- **Productively managing time** is a skill that great men and women learn. ("Productively" modifies "managing" and "time" is the direct object of "managing.")
- **His skillful explaining of grammar** made my life easier. ("Skillful" modifies "explaining.")

*A special note: an adjective with a gerund is stylistically pleasant.

- **Giving him money** is probably not the best idea. ("Him" is the indirect object; "Money" = direct object)

Try these:

- Writing essays requires time and effort.
- Cultivating the mind is as necessary as eating food for the body.
- Nothing gets done by complaining.

19.5 The gerund phrase includes all objects and modifiers.

- **Traveling lightly** is wise when you go hiking.
- **Looking for your ring on the beach** is an impossible task. ("On the beach" is a prepositional phrase, but it is an adverbial phrase that modifies the gerund, "looking.")
- **By riding your bicycle on the right side of the road**, you limit the dangers of oncoming traffic.
- I do not like **wasting the time of others**.
- Nicholas might be in trouble **for failing to hand in his homework**. ("To hand" is an infinitive. We will get to infinitives in a subsequent section.)

20. PARTICIPLES I

20.1 Participles are verbal adjectives. As a verb, a participle can take modifiers and objects. As an adjective, a participle must modify a noun or pronoun.

- Plowing the fields, the farmer was exhausted. ("Field" is the direct object of "plowing," and "plowing" modifies "farmer.")
- Diligently plowing the fields, the farmer was exhausted. ("Diligently" modifies plowing, "fields" is the direct object of "plowing," and "plowing" modifies "farmer.")

20.2 There are two kinds of participles.

- Present participles end in -ing. For example: giving, running, and eating.
- Pay special attention to distinguish present participles from gerunds. Participles are verbal adjectives and gerunds are verbal nouns.
- Past participles use a helping word and do not end in –ing. For example: Having run the marathon, the woman was exhausted. With practice you will locate past participles with little problem.
- Past participles can end in -d, -ed, -n, -en, or even -t. For example, given, run, eaten, and lent (past participle of lend).

20.3 All participles modify nouns or pronouns. To find out what a participle modifies, ask:

- Who or what is ________________________?
- Who or what was or has________________________?

If this question cannot be answered in a sensible way, there is no participle.

- The man swimming in the lake is an old classmate. Who or what is swimming? The man.
- The man having swum in the lake felt a chill down his spine. Who or what has swum? The man.
- The swimming pool is a sight to behold. Who or what is swimming? The swimming pool can't swim. So, "swimming" is an adjective.
- Astonished by the sights and sounds of the amusement park, the boy stood speechless and agape. Who or what was astonished? The boy.
- Having run its course, the Black Death took a huge toll of the population in the 14th century. Who or what has run? The Black Death.

20.4 Helpful Patterns:

- Introductory Participles. Swimming, the fish hit the tank.
- Participle before the word it modifies. Here the participle functions like an adjective. The broken mouse is next to the computer.
- Participle after the word it modifies. The man running to catch the train fell.

20.5 The difference between gerunds and participles can be tricky. The best way to tell the difference between the two is by examining the grammatical function of each word. Gerunds are verbal nouns; participles are verbal adjectives. Examine these sentences carefully.

- Leaving New York was a relief.
- Leaving New York, I was relieved.
- Seeing the world in my twenties was one of my main goals in life.
- Seeing the world in my twenties, I accomplished one of my main goals in life.
- I loved running the marathon.
- Hitting a ninety mile an hour pitch made the high school student feel special.
- Throwing down his glove, the batter charged the mound.

21. PARTICIPLES II

21.1 Participles can have more than one word.

- The man **having seen** the bird felt happy.

21.2 Passive participles need a helping word.

- Sisyphus exhausted himself having been forced to carry the rock. (Three words—having been forced)
- Having been demoted, the captain felt shame and regret. (Three words—having been demoted)
- Having been chastised, the boys reformed their ways. (Three words—having been chastised)
- Having been seen by the enemies in the forest, the general decided to move deeper into the forest. (Three words—having been seen)
- The sunbather fell asleep being baked by the sun. (Two words—being baked)

21.3 Progressive tenses use participles with helping verbs.

- Auxiliary verb + verb of being + participle create progressive tenses. When this happens, consider it a verb.
- Nancy was hoping for a miracle. (Progressive tense) We can make this into a simple past tense by writing the sentence: "Nancy hoped for a miracle."

- Monica will be eating Italian food for lunch and dinner. (Progressive future) We can also rewrite this sentence: "Monica will eat Italian food for lunch and dinner."
- George was swimming with the sharks at the water park. We can also rewrite this sentence: "George swam with the sharks at the water park."
- Perfect / Pluperfect / Future perfect tenses with auxiliary verb (have / had / will have) + past participle.
- Professor Hamilton has purchased three coins for the University's collection. (Has purchased = perfect tense = auxiliary verb + past participle)
- She had completed the project. (Had completed = pluperfect tense = auxiliary verb + past participle)
- The miser had saved all his money, but he tragically died before he used any of it. (Had saved = pluperfect tense = auxiliary verb + past participle)
- Luke will have married the girl of his dreams by adulthood. (Will have married = future perfect tense = auxiliary verb + past participle)

21.4 The Passive voice also uses a participle. Here is the rule. Verb of being + past participle = passive voice of a verb.

- Jennifer and her friends were seen in a cab going down Madison Avenue. (Were seen = passive verb = verb of being + past participle)
- The boy was smitten with love when he saw the giant Gummy Bear. (Was smitten = passive verb = verb of being + past participle)
- She was carried on a litter through the crowd. (Was carried = passive verb = verb of being + past participle)
- The desk was scratched by a pen. (Was scratched = passive verb = verb of being + past participle)

21.5 Dangling participles:

Participles must be placed in the correct place in the sentence; otherwise, the sentence will be nonsensical. A good general rule of thumb is to keep the participle close to the word it modifies. Here are some examples of misplaced participles:

- Professor Grassi saw the dissertation glancing to his left. This sentence says that the dissertation is glancing.
- Picking fleas off his mate, the scientists recorded the apes.
- Foaming at the mouth, Atticus shot the rabid dog.
- Managing such a complex city, the boy respected the mayor.

22. INFINITIVES I

22.1 An infinitive is composed of "to" plus the verb. It is usually used as a noun. It can also be an adjective or adverb.

- An infinitive is easy to identify. "To" + the "Verb" = infinitive.
- Examples: to run, to see, to eat, to be, to sing, to study, etc.
- It is important to note that "to" is not a preposition. Prepositions have a noun or pronoun as an object, never a verb.

22.2 Infinitive as a noun:

- As a noun, an infinitive can function as subject, direct object, predicate nominative, and appositive.
- **To win the game** was my desire. To win = subject.
- I love **to eat**. To eat = direct object.
- My ambition in life is **to hold one world record**. To hold one world record = predicate nominative.
- John's accomplishment, **to eat ten slices of pizza**, made him famous at school (and sick). To eat ten slices of pizza = appositive.
- It would make me sick **to eat the meatloaf**. This sentence can be rewritten: "To eat the meatloaf would make me sick." To eat the meatloaf = subject.

22.3 Infinitive as an adjective:

- Like an adjective, an infinitive can be used to describe a noun.
- An adjectival infinitive always follows the noun it describes.
- This is the best pizza **to eat**. What pizza? The answer is: the best pizza to eat. You can clearly see that the infinitive is adjectival. A few more examples will make this point clear.
- This is the video **to watch** if you want to learn about carpentry.
- Whenever I take the subway, I carry a book **to read**, just in case I get caught in traffic.
- He lacked the stamina **to finish** the quest.
- Notice that all the infinitives follow the noun it modifies.

22.4 Infinitive as adverb:

- An easy way to identify an adverbial infinitive is to see if you can replace the infinitive with "in order to." If you can do this, you have an adverbial infinitive.
- She practiced the cello all night to perform well. The sentence can be rewritten: She practiced all night in order to perform well.
- We exercised to get stronger. The sentence can be rewritten: We exercised in order to get stronger.
- To win the geography competition, the boy memorized the atlas. The sentence can be rewritten: In order to win the geography competition, the boy memorized the atlas.
- Notice that introductory dependent clauses need a comma.

22.5 Verbal quality of an infinitive:

- Since an infinitive has a verbal force, it can take an object.
- To win the race, the boy exercised after school. "Race" is the object of the infinitive. The infinitive "to win" is adverbial.
- I love to eat all foods. "Foods" is the object of "to eat," which is the direct object of the sentence.
- To give him an answer, I had to read three articles. What is "him" in this sentence? If you said it was an indirect object, you are correct. Infinitives can have indirect objects as well.

23. INFINITIVES II

23.1 Complementary Infinitives:

A complementary infinitive completes the meaning of certain verbs—able, ought, dare, desire.

- He is able to do well.
- She ought to repay the money she borrowed.
- They will dare to sail the sea.
- Who desires to train for the marathon with Jessie?

Latin does the same: *possum, soleo, volo, nolo, cupio,* etc.

- *Possum arborem videre.* I am able to see a tree.

23.2 Infinitive phrases can have a "subject," but the whole phrase functions as the direct object.

- Consider the following sentence. "She asked him to carry the desk."
- The infinitive phrase consists of "him to carry the desk."
- By using the replacement method, it is clear that the infinitive phrase is the direct object. We can rewrite the sentence. "She asked it."
- Within the infinitive phrase, the word, "him" functions as the "subject," though it is in the object case, and the infinitive "to carry" functions as the verb. "The desk" is the object of the infinitive.

- Try this example. "They wanted her to be the leader."
- Use the replacement method. "They wanted it." "It" replaces "her to be the leader."
- "Her" is the subject of the infinitive phrase. Notice it is in the object case.
- The infinitive "to be" functions as the verb.
- "Leader" is a predicate nominative because of the linking verb.
- Some verbs that follow this pattern are advise, encourage, tell, order, force. Once you see the pattern, these sentences will become second nature.
- In Latin, certain verbs follow his pattern as well (*iubeo* and *cogo*).
- *Milites coegerunt viros villas relinquere.* The soldiers forced the men to leave their farmhouses.
- Indirect discourse is another example. *Caesar dixit milites flumen videre.* Caesar said that the soldiers saw the river.

23.3 Split infinitives:

When grammar teachers tell you not to split infinitives, they are saying that there should be no adverb between "to" and the "verb."

- To run quickly vs. to quickly run.
- To study diligently vs. to diligently study.
- To sit calmly vs. to calmly sit.
- The latter are split infinitives.

The reason why some teachers say that you should not split an infinitive is rooted in Latin. The infinitive of a Latin verb (second principal part) cannot be split.

- *Laudare, monere, cedere, audire, pungare*
- Can you split infinitives? Yes, but if it can be avoided, especially in formal writing, it is a good idea.

23.4 Some infinitives drop "to."

- She **made** me **do** the assignment again!
- When she asked me for permission, I **let** her **go**.

23.5 Infinitives have tense.

- To see (present)
- To have seen (perfect)
- Unlike in Latin, English does not have a future infinitive.

VERBAL TEST:

I. Underline all verbals, drawing arrows where appropriate.

1. The birdwatcher spotted the resting bird while walking in Central Park, but when he dropped his binoculars, the bird, startled, flew away.
2. Being late for the meeting is not the worst thing to do, but you should apologize.
3. There was once a prince who wished to marry a princess; but then she must be a real Princess. He traveled all over the world in hopes of finding such a lady; but there was always something wrong. Hans Andersen, "The Real Princess"

4. The delivery man was standing in the rain waiting for someone to buzz him in, but no one was home.
5. The jar of clay with the ancient manuscripts was waiting for the last two thousand years to be discovered.
6. The bruised pride of the fighter was not a pleasant sight to behold.
7. After a century of wielding economic and political power, America's gas giants face a reckoning for causing untold problems.
8. Small hamlets, struggling to keep their businesses open, have resorted to online models to compete with national chains.
9. Raging against technology, the professor concluded that machines will not only take over key industries but also make people less prepared to adapt to a changing world.
10. Every time our brains learns a new subject, neurons create new pathways, making our brain more resilient to decay.

II. Identity the underlined words.

"And over the grass at the roadside a land turtle crawled, **<u>turning aside for nothing</u>**, dragging his high-domed shell over the grass. His hard legs and yellow-nailed feet threshed slowly through the grass, not really **<u>walking</u>**, but boosting and **<u>dragging</u>** his shell along. The barley beards slid off his shell, and the clover burrs fell on him and rolled to the **ground.** His horny beak was partly open, and his fierce, humorous eyes, under brows **like fingernails**, stared straight **ahead.** He came over the grass leaving a **beaten** trail behind him, and the hill, **which was the highway embankment**, reared up ahead of him. For a moment he stopped, his head held high. He blinked and looked up and down.

At last he started to climb the embankment. Front clawed feet reached forward but did not touch. The hind feet kicked his shell along, and it **scraped** on the grass, and on the gravel. As the embankment grew steeper and steeper, the more frantic were the efforts of the land turtle. Pushing hind legs strained and slipped, boosting the shell along, and the horny head protruded **as far as the neck could stretch**. Little by little the shell slid up the embankment until at last a parapet cut straight across its line of march, **the shoulder of the road**, a concrete wall four inches high. **As though they worked independently** the hind legs pushed the shell against the wall. The head upraised and peered over the wall to the broad smooth plain of cement. Now the hands, braced on top of the wall, **strained** and lifted, and the shell came slowly up and rested its front **end** on the wall. For a moment the turtle rested. A red ant ran into the shell, into the soft skin inside the shell, and suddenly head and legs snapped in, and the armored tail clamped in **sideways**. The red ant was crushed between body and legs. And one head of wild oats was clamped into the shell by a front leg. For a long moment the turtle lay still, and then the neck crept out and the old humorous frowning eyes looked about and the legs and tail came out. The back legs went to work, straining like elephant legs, and the shell tipped to an angle **so that the front legs scratched at the pavement**, and it was up. But the head of wild oats was held by its stem around the front legs."

John Steinbeck, *The Grapes of Wrath*

FIVE

PUNCTUATION

24. PERIODS

24.1 A period ends a sentence.

- It all ends here.
- Stand firm.
- Let's eat.
- Go.

24.2 Do not mistake a dependent clause for an independent one. Dependent clauses do not have periods because they are not complete sentences.

- When I left my previous job...
- If I skip breakfast...
- When I left my previous job, I took a long break.
- If I skip breakfast, hunger pangs hit me around noon.

24.3 Initials require periods.

- G. K. Chesterton said: "Misers get up early in the morning; and burglars, I am informed, get up the night before."
- C. S. Lewis once stated that the task of the modern educator is not to cut down jungles but irrigate deserts.

24.4 Abbreviations for states do not need periods.

- I used to live in NJ, but now I live in NY.
- I love CA.

24.5 URL addresses receive a period at the end of a sentence.

- I love and hate www.amazon.com.

24.6 The period comes within a quote.

- "It often requires more courage to dare to do right than to fear to do wrong." Abraham Lincoln
- In British English, the period come after the quotation mark, which makes more sense.

24.7 Omit a period to end a sentence if a period is already present.

- I read a great article about John F. Kennedy Jr.
- I love chemistry, biology, history, Latin, etc.

25. COMMAS

25.1 Commas separate. Mastering comma rules can be tricky, but with practice you will grow in confidence. Once you master the basic rules, you will realize that there is stylistic flexibility.

25.2 Items in a series require a comma.

- He loves to study Greek, Latin, and Sanskrit.
- She visited Mongolia, Kazakhstan, and Kyrgyzstan.
- The boys studied vigorously, diligently, and enthusiastically.
- He is a triathlete. He swam 2.4 miles, rode his bike for 112 miles, and ran 26.2 miles.

25.3 The Oxford or serial comma offers greater clarity.

- I saw my teachers, Martha, and Mary.
- I saw my teachers, Martha and Mary.
- There is a difference between the two. In the first sentence, I saw my teachers and two other people (Mary and Martha).
- In the second sentence, there is ambiguity. Martha and Mary can be the names of my teachers. In this case, Marth and Mary are appositives.
- By using the Oxford comma, ambiguity is eliminated.

25.4 Phrases can be in a series as well.

- Paul lived in Rome, next to Rome, and outside of Rome.

- The Romans had a form of government for the people, on behalf of the people, and by the people.

25.5 Introductory phrases or words may have a comma.

- On Monday, I get up extra early.
- On Monday I get up extra early.
- In the stillness of the dawn, I meditate.
- Readability and clarity will dictate whether a comma is needed.

25.6 Commas with independent clauses.

- I saw the movie on Friday, but my mother saw it on Thursday.
- The Sixth Grade loved *Tom Sawyer*, and the Seventh Grade loved *Beowulf*.
- I know that you will do whatever you want, so do it.
- She had a great year in Spanish class, and she will do even better next year.
- We love it, and we are not ashamed to say it.

25.7 When the sentence is short, the comma may be omitted.

- Daphne runs and Apollo chases.

25.8 Compound verbs with a single subject do not need a comma.

- She ran for president and won by the landslide.
- The athlete scored the goal in the final seconds of the game and immediately ran a victory lap.
- The teacher looked at the students with cold eyes but smiled throughout the class.

25.9 Introductory dependent clauses require a comma.

- When I exercise, I am famished.
- Since the leaves are turning colors, I can tell fall is approaching.
- Unless you save your allowance, you will never be able to buy the boxed set of *The Chronicles of Narnia.*

25.10 A dependent clause after a main clause does not require a comma.

- I am famished when I exercise.
- I can tell fall is approaching since the leaves are turning colors.
- You will never be able to buy the boxed set of *The Chronicles of Narnia* unless you save your allowance.

25.11 Appositives are set off by commas.

- David, the chairman, will attend the gala.
- My favorite car, a blue Maserati, is out of my league.

25.12 Nonessential adjective clauses / relative clauses need commas.

- Soldiers, who are in our town, are trained to defend people.
- Jeff, who is my cousin, lives in San Francisco.

25.13 Essential adjectival clauses do not have commas.

- The book that I love is on my bedroom dresser.

- The person that wins the contest will gain the prize.
- Generally speaking, "that" introduces an essential clause.

25.14 Inverted adjective / noun pairs often use a comma.

- The hero, tall and sturdy, possessed a fearless mien.
- The tall and sturdy hero possessed a fearless mien.

25.15 Direct addresses are set off by commas.

- Hey man, watch it.
- Kid, I am talking to you.

25.16 Elliptical constructions.

- He won the battle; she, the war.

EXERCISES:

Punctuate with commas and periods. Cross out misplaced commas.

1. Because the Lower School has too much energy the teachers don't mind giving an hour recess and two hours of physical education.
2. Mom can you please send my books first thing in the morning?
3. Matt who won the Nobel Peace Prize in science stole the formula from his Middle School science teacher Dr. Long.

4. The sailor tall and defiant stared into the sea eating a bag of Pirate's Booty.

5. The rumor that Dr Kim is a spy may have some validity; I heard him speak Russian Finnish and Mandarin.

6. Because I was so hungry I ate four eggs, three pancakes, and a steak.

7. Socrates sees himself as a gadfly that the gods have chosen to provoke Athens a great and noble steed that is slow to move on account of its size. At times he fastens on them when they are slumbering but his sting is for their good so that they would live a life of virtue. He will continue even if it leads to his death.

8. The study of war a common topic among historians of the early 1900 is no longer popular these days.

9. The pizza is here! Let's eat grandma.

10. John K Dickerson became the head of the department, when the former chair was promoted to dean.

11. The editor mentioned the difficulties of the economy the problems of capitalism and the challenges of socialism.

12. Since the departments merged there is little distinction between classics, history and religion.

13. On the high mountainous plateau the tourists can see for fifty miles.

14. Although he is a graduate with a PhD from Yale which is in C.T. he now lives in Singapore a country that is extremely far from New Haven.
15. My dentist ran four triathlons, and is preparing for another in the spring.

EXERCISES:

Punctuate with commas.

1. "Grushenka lived in the busiest part of town near the cathedral square in a house belonging to the widow of the merchant Morozov from whom she rented a small wooden cottage. The widow's house was large, stone, two-storied old, and extremely unattractive. The owner an old woman lived a secluded life there with her two nieces also quite elderly spinsters." Fyodor Dostoevsky, *Brothers Karamazov*
2. "'But you've already forgiven him' Alyosha said, smiling. 'Yes I've forgiven him,' Grushenka said meaningly. 'What a base heart! To my base heart!' She suddenly snatched a glass from the table drank it in one gulp held it up and smashed it as hard as she could on the floor. The glass shattered and tinkled. A certain cruel line flashed in her smile." Fyodor Dostoevsky, *Brothers Karamazov*
3. "Oared warships of which the trireme is the most famous lie at the heart of the Greek Hellenistic and Roman story

as it unfolds from Homer to Constantine. In the seventh and sixth centuries BC oared galleys took Greek colonists from their mother cities to all parts of the Mediterranean and the Black Sea. In 480 BC a great Persian armada was defeated by a much smaller Greek fleet in the narrow waters between Attica and the island of Salamis. Athens' ensuing maritime supremacy was founded on the crucial role which she played in that famous victory. The skilled use of the triremes enabled her to win, and for some decades to keep, the hegemony over some, at least, of her former Greek allies." J. S. Morrison, J. E. Coates, and N. B. Rankov, *The Athenian Trireme*

This is how the authors punctuated their texts.

1. "Grushenka lived in the busiest part of town, near the cathedral square, in a house belonging to the widow of the merchant Morozov, from whom she rented a small wooden cottage. The widow's house was large, stone, two-storied, old, and extremely unattractive. The owner, an old woman, lived a secluded life there with her two nieces, also quite elderly spinsters." Fyodor Dostoevsky, *Brothers Karamazov*
2. "'But you've already forgiven him,' Alyosha said, smiling. 'Yes, I've forgiven him,' Grushenka said meaningly. 'What a base heart! To my base heart!' She suddenly snatched a glass from the table, drank it in one gulp, held it up, and smashed

it as hard as she could on the floor. The glass shattered and tinkled. A certain cruel line flashed in her smile." Fyodor Dostoevsky, *Brothers Karamazov*

3. "Oared warships, of which the trireme is the most famous, lie at the heart of the Greek, Hellenistic, and Roman story as it unfolds from Homer to Constantine. In the seventh and sixth centuries BC, oared galleys took Greek colonists from their mother cities to all parts of the Mediterranean and the Black Sea. In 480 BC a great Persian armada was defeated by a much smaller Greek fleet in the narrow waters between Attica and the island of Salamis. Athens' ensuing maritime supremacy was founded on the crucial role which she played in that famous victory. The skilled use of the triremes enabled her to win, and for some decades to keep, the hegemony over some, at least, of her former Greek allies." J. S. Morrison, J. E. Coates, and N. B. Rankov, *The Athenian Trireme*

26. SEMICOLONS AND COLONS

26.1 Semicolons connect two closely related independent clauses.

- She just finished the New York City Marathon; she will run the Boston Marathon next year.
- I love movies; *Lord of the Rings* is my favorite.
- Mr. Wilson loves New York City; Toledo is a close second.

26.2 Conjunctive adverbs can be used with semicolons and independent clauses.

- The boy was not afraid to take the cookies; therefore, he was begging for trouble.
- She prepared for months; so, all agree that she will do well.
- The Spartans lost the battle; therefore, they retreated.
- There are other conjunctive adverbs: however, therefore, indeed, hence, and thus.

26.3 Use semicolons when commas won't do.

- I lived in New Haven, Connecticut; Philadelphia, Pennsylvania; and New York, New York.
- The scholar trying to prove the goodwill of the Romans stated that they only fought defensive war; placed religious piety above wealth; sought peace if it could be achieved.

26.4 Use a colon to begin a list at the end of a sentence.

- Here is what I have in my bag: apples, oranges, two pens, and one book.

26.5 Use a colon to set off a long quotation:

Ramsay MacMullen, the great Roman historian, argued that supernatural acts caused the early church to grow:

Clearly some very large part of the population, one region in the province Pontus, was won over to the church by Gregory the Wonderworker in specific and identifiable decades—our only surviving account of any such event, however many others there may or must have been just like it. He succeeded perhaps in part through speaking publicly to groups. He is shown speaking like that but confirming or instructing. No conversions are said to result. Rather, and expressly, conversions result from his supernatural acts; and, by implication and by position in the narrative, they are presented as the cause of the whole grand picture of his success in his campaigns against demonic hosts.

26.6 Use a colon to summarize or explain the preceding clause.

- This is the best bank in the city: it is open late, it offers free checking, and it does not charge ATM fees.

EXERCISES:

Punctuate with semicolons and colons.

1. Greed motivates many people businesses and governments charities are not an exception.
2. Edith Hamilton once wrote "Demosthenes is a strange figure as he stands in the Assembly in the fourth-century, pouring forth words of fire. He belongs to another age he is a hundred years too late..."
3. My parents moved around a lot. They used to live in Newark, New Jersey, Rome, Italy, and Beijing China.
4. There comes a time when we must dip into the emergency funds however, that time is not now.

Write a compound-complex sentence that uses a semicolon.

____

____

____

Write a compound-complex sentence that uses a colon.

____

____

____

27. QUESTION MARKS

27.1 The question mark asks a question.

- Who did that?
- Why did they take the books?
- Where will the children stay?
- Whose book is it?

27.2 Questions marks replace a comma.

- "Are there enough snacks for all our guests?" the teacher asked.
- "When will we arrive at the park?" asked the children.
- "What can be done?" he wondered.
- "Why am I here?" she asked herself.

27.3 Question marks also replace a period.

- The dentist said, "My buddy, do you really brush your teeth twice a day?"
- He asked under his breath why can't I be the king?

27.4 Rhetorical questions can take a question mark, period, or an exclamation point. The context is key.

- Well, what do you know?
- Why don't you take hike!
- Well, how about that.
- Isn't she lovely.
- Who can blame him!

28. APOSTROPHES

28.1 Apostrophes have two main functions.

- They indicate possession (think of a possessive genitive in Latin).
- They show that a letter or letters have been omitted.

28.2 An apostrophe can indicate possession.

- The horse's tail was brown.
- The tail of the horse was brown.
- Joseph's dilemma is not as serious as Michael's.
- Sword's hilt
- America's wealth

28.3 With words that end in s, add an apostrophe plus "s."

- I can't help but covet Mr. Jones's farm.
- The canvass's size and color are perfect for Mr. Popa's art project.
- My boss's suit was two sizes too small, and he was wearing his son's tie.
- James's triumph is a testimony to his perseverance.

28.4 Plural nouns that end in "s" only receive an apostrophe.

- I accidentally ate the cats' food. It could have used hot sauce.
- The boys' blazers were left on the bus.

28.5 Plural of family names do not receive an apostrophe.

- The Reeds are wonderful.
- The Joneses are coming to the party tonight.
- I saw the Walshes at Central Park.

28.6 "Its" is a possessive like hers or his; "it's" is a contraction of it and is.

- It's nine in the morning, and I am late for school.
- Windex is amazing. Its properties solve all problems: streaks, dirt, acne, and so much more.

28.7 Omission of numbers

- I am a child of the '80s.

28.8 Contractions require apostrophes.

- I shouldn't have eaten that extra pie of pizza.
- You don't want Mr. Jones to come, do you?

EXERCISES:

Punctuate with apostrophes.

1. If we cant make the train, then we will have to drive.
2. When the animals couldnt take Joness oppression, they took over the farm.
3. Its a matter of time.

4. Thieves possess peoples goods.

5. During the 30s, Americans went through many challenges.

6. Did William Shakespeare really write: “Whats in a name?”

7. The cafés ambiance reminded me of Paris.

8. Animals are wont to attack when they are scared, but they usually wont attack when they are secure.

9. The branchs shade gave relief to Jonah.

10. Atticus says that you cant punish the children for the fathers faults.

11. “He is a great observer and he looks
Quite through the deeds of men: he loves no plays,
As thou dost, Antony; he hears no music;
Seldom he smiles, and smiles in such a sort
As if he mockd himself and scornd his spirit
That could be moved to smile at anything.
Such men as he be never at heart’s ease
Whiles they behold a greater than themselves,
And therefore are they very dangerous.”

Shakespeare, *Julius Caesar*

Punctuate with Apostrophes
There are five missing apostrophes.

He said, "Im Charles Baker Harris. I can read."

"So what?" I said.

Jem wanted to get a better look at him, so he said, "Why dont you come over, Charles Baker Harris."

"Folks call me Dill, "he said, struggling to fit under the fence. Dill told us he was from Mississippi, but he was spending the summer with his aunt Rachel. He had seen a bunch of movies, so he described them to us, and we spent the next days acting them out. He was very creative, and always had good ideas. We eventually got tired of recreating Dracula and other stories. Thats when Dills fascination with the Radley house began.

The Radley house had sagging shingles, and a drooping porch. The grass was too high, and the paint had turned gray and dingy. Even in the long, hot summer, the doors were shut up tight. There was a rumor that it was haunted. People said "Boo" Radley went out at night and peeped in people's windows. That he breathed on flowers and they froze instantly. They said he committed little crimes in the night but not one ever saw him.

The history of the story is that Arthur, "Boo", got into a bad crowd in high school. They swore, fought, and got into real trouble when they locked a court officer in the outhouse (bathroom). Boos father was so strict that the judge let him take Boo home, and no one had seen him since. Years later, the story goes, Boo was making a scrapbook out of articles from the Maycomb Tribune when he stabbed his father with a pair of scissors and kept right on cutting. Mr. Radley was not a nice man.

Harper Lee, *To Kill a Mockingbird*

29. EXCLAMATION POINTS

29.1 Exclamation points are used to express heights of emotion, usually in an interjection or an imperative.

- Zoinks!
- Zip it, all of you!
- Run from here now!
- Watch it!

29.2 Exclamation points can replace a comma.

- "Zoinks!" Scooby said.
- "This is awesome!" he shouted.
- "Nothing there!" said Peter, and they all trooped out again—all except Lucy. She stayed behind because she thought it would be worth while trying the door of the wardrobe, even though she felt almost sure that it would be locked. To her surprise it opened quite easily, and two moth-balls dropped out. C. S. Lewis, *The Lion, the Witch and the Wardrobe*

29.3 Exclamation points can replace a period.

- The marines shouted "booyah!"
- He said, "Watch it!"

29.4 Use exclamation points sparingly and do not use multiple exclamation points.

- I love it!!!!
- Are you serious?!?!
- Really????
- Moderation is a virtue. Good writing rarely uses exclamation points.

29.5 Examples:

- "'Now!' he said aloud and struck hard with both hands, gained a yard of line and then struck again and again, swinging with each arm alternately on the cord with all the strength of his arms and the pivoted weight of his body." Ernest Hemingway, *The Old Man and the Sea*

- "But is this simply part of the order of nature? Is it because this land of ours is so poor that it cannot afford a decent life to those who dwell upon it? No, comrades, a thousand times no! The soil of England is fertile, its climate is good, it is capable of affording food in abundance to an enormously greater number of animals than now inhabit it. This single farm of ours would support a dozen horses, twenty cows, hundreds of sheep—and all of them living in a comfort and a dignity that are now almost beyond our imagining. Why then do we continue in this miserable condition? Because nearly the whole of the produce of our labour is stolen from us by human beings. There, comrades, is the answer to all our problems. It is summed up in a single word—Man. Man is the only real enemy we have. Remove Man from the scene, and the root cause of hunger and overwork is abolished forever." George Orwell, *Animal Farm*

EXERCISES:

All punctuations marks have been removed except final periods and question marks. Punctuate this excerpt.

Man is the only creature that consumes without producing. He does not give milk he does not lay eggs he is too weak to pull the plough he cannot run fast enough to catch rabbits. Yet he is lord of all the animals. He sets them to work he gives back to them the bare minimum that will prevent them from starving and the rest he keeps for himself. Our labour tills the soil our dung fertilises it and yet there is not one of us that owns more than his bare skin. You cows that I see before me how many thousands of gallons of milk have you given during this last year. And what has happened to that milk which should have been breeding up sturdy calves. Every drop of it has gone down the throats of our enemies.

And you hens how many eggs have you laid in this last year, and how many of those eggs ever hatched into chickens? The rest have all gone to market to bring in money for Jones and his men. And you Clover where are those four foals you bore who should have been the support and pleasure of your old age. Each was sold at a year old–you will never see one of them again. In return for your four confinements and all your labour in the fields what have you ever had except your bare rations and a stall?

And even the miserable lives we lead are not allowed to reach their natural span. For myself I do not grumble for I am one of the lucky ones. I am twelve years old and have had over four hundred children. Such is the natural life of a pig. But no animal escapes the cruel knife in the end. You young porkers who are sitting in front of me every one of you will scream your lives out at the block within a year. To that horror we all must come–cows, pigs, hens, sheep everyone. Even the horses and the dogs have no better fate. You, Boxer the very day that those great muscles of yours lose their power, Jones will sell you to the knacker, who will cut your throat and boil you down for the foxhounds. As for the dogs, when they grow old and toothless Jones ties a brick round their necks and drowns them in the nearest pond.

Is it not crystal clear, then, comrades, that all the evils of this life of ours spring from the tyranny of human beings? Only get rid of Man, and the produce of our labour would be our own. A1most overnight we could become rich and free. What then must we do? Why work night and day body and soul for the overthrow of the human race! That is my message to you comrades Rebellion! I do not know when that Rebellion will come, it might be in a week or in a hundred years, but I know as surely as I see this straw beneath my feet that sooner or later justice will be done. Fix your eyes on that comrades throughout the short remainder of your lives! and above all, pass on this message of mine to those who come after you, so that future generations shall carry on the struggle until it is victorious.

And remember comrades your resolution must never falter. No argument must lead you astray. Never listen when they tell you that Man and the animals have a common interest, that the prosperity of the one is the prosperity of the others. It is all lies Man serves the interests of no creature except himself. And among us animals let there be perfect unity perfect comradeship in the struggle. All men are enemies? All animals are comrades.

George Orwell, *Animal Farm*

This is how George Orwell punctuated the text.

'Man is the only creature that consumes without producing. He does not give milk, he does not lay eggs, he is too weak to pull the plough, he cannot run fast enough to catch rabbits. Yet he is lord of all the animals. He sets them to work, he gives back to them the bare minimum that will prevent them from starving, and the rest he keeps for himself. Our labour tills the soil, our dung fertilises it, and yet there is not one of us that owns more than his bare skin.

You cows that I see before me, how many thousands of gallons of milk have you given during this last year? And what has happened to that milk which should have been breeding up sturdy calves? Every drop of it has gone down the throats of our enemies. And you hens, how many eggs have you laid in this last year, and how many of those eggs ever hatched into chickens? The rest have all gone to market to bring in money for Jones and his men. And you, Clover, where are those four foals you bore, who should have been the support and pleasure of your old age? Each was sold at a year old — you will never see one of them again. In return for your four confinements and all your labour in the fields, what have you ever had except your bare rations and a stall?

'And even the miserable lives we lead are not allowed to reach their natural span. For myself I do not grumble, for I am one of the lucky ones. I am twelve years old and have had over four hundred children. Such is the natural life of a pig. But no animal escapes the cruel knife in the end. You young porkers who are sitting in front of me, every one of you will scream your lives out at the block within a year. To that horror we all must come—cows, pigs, hens, sheep, everyone. Even the horses and the dogs have no better fate. You, Boxer, the very day that those great muscles of yours lose their power, Jones will sell you to the knacker, who will cut your throat and boil you down for the foxhounds. As for the dogs, when they grow old and toothless, Jones ties a brick round their necks and drowns them in the nearest pond.

'Is it not crystal clear, then, comrades, that all the evils of this life of ours spring from the tyranny of human beings? Only get rid of Man, and the produce of our labour would be our own. A1most overnight we could become rich and free. What then must we do? Why, work night and day, body and soul, for the overthrow of the human race! That is my message to you, comrades: Rebellion! I do not know when that Rebellion will come, it might be in a week or in a hundred years, but I know, as surely as I see this straw beneath my feet, that sooner or later justice will be done. Fix your eyes on that, comrades, throughout the short remainder of your lives! And above all, pass on this message of mine to those who come after you, so that future generations shall carry on the struggle until it is victorious.

'And remember, comrades, your resolution must never falter. No argument must lead you astray. Never listen when they tell you that Man and the animals have a common interest, that the prosperity of the one is the prosperity of the others. It is all lies. Man serves the interests of no creature except himself. And among us animals let there be perfect unity, perfect comradeship in the struggle. All men are enemies. All animals are comrades.'

George Orwell, *Animal Farm*

EXERCISES:

All punctuations marks have been removed except final periods and question marks. Punctuate this excerpt.

The second service that one should perform for another in a Christian community is that of active helpfulness. This means initially simple assistance in trifling external matters. There is a multitude of these things wherever people live together. Nobody is too good for the meanest service. One who worries about the loss of time that such petty outward acts of helpfulness entail is usually taking the importance of his own career too solemnly.

We must be ready to allow ourselves to be interrupted by God. God will be constantly crossing our paths and cancelling our plans by sending us people with claims and petitions. We may pass them by, preoccupied with our more important tasks, as the priest passed by the man who had fallen among thieves, perhaps—reading the Bible. When we do that we pass by the visible sign of the Cross raised athwart our path to show us that, not our way but God's way must be done. It is a strange fact that Christians and even ministers frequently consider their work so important and urgent that they will allow nothing to disturb them. They think they are doing God a service in this, but actually they are disdaining Gods 'crooked yet straight path.' They do not want a life that is crossed and balked. But it is part of the discipline of humility that we must not spare our hand where it can perform a service and that we do not assume that our schedule is our own to manage but allow it to be arranged by God.

In the monastery his vow of obedience to the abbot deprives the monk of the right to dispose of his own time. In evangelical community life free service to ones brother takes the place of the vow. Only where hands are not too good for deeds of love and mercy in everyday helpfulness can the mouth joyfully and convincingly proclaim the message of Gods love and mercy.

Dietrich Bonhoeffer, *Life Together*

This is how Dietrich Bonhoeffer punctuated his text.

The second service that one should perform for another in a Christian community is that of active helpfulness. This means, initially, simple assistance in trifling, external matters. There is a multitude of these things wherever people live together. Nobody is too good for the meanest service. One who worries about the loss of time that such petty, outward acts of helpfulness entail is usually taking the importance of his own career too solemnly.

We must be ready to allow ourselves to be interrupted by God. God will be constantly crossing our paths and cancelling our plans by sending us people with claims and petitions. We may pass them by, preoccupied with our more important tasks, as the priest passed by the man who had fallen among thieves, perhaps—reading the Bible. When we do that, we pass by the visible sign of the Cross raised athwart our path to show us that, not our way, but God's way must be done. It is a strange fact that Christians and even ministers frequently consider their work so important and urgent that they will allow nothing to disturb them. They think they are doing God a service in this, but actually they are disdaining God's 'crooked yet straight path.' They do not want a life that is crossed and balked. But it is part of the discipline of humility that we must not spare our hand where it can perform a service and that we do not assume that our schedule is our own to manage but allow it to be arranged by God.

In the monastery his vow of obedience to the abbot deprives the monk of the right to dispose of his own time. In evangelical community life, free service to one's brother takes the place of the vow. Only where hands are not too good for deeds of love and mercy in everyday helpfulness can the mouth joyfully and convincingly proclaim the message of God's love and mercy.

Dietrich Bonhoeffer, *Life Together*

EXERCISE:

All punctuations marks have been removed except final periods and question marks. Punctuate this excerpt.

Masson wanted to have a swim at once but his wife and Raymond were disinclined to move. So only the three of us Marie Masson and myself went down to the beach. Marie promptly plunged in but Masson and I waited for a bit. He was rather slow of speech and had I noticed a habit of saying "and what's more" between his phrases—even when the second added nothing really to the first. Talking of Marie, he said "She's an awfully pretty girl and whats more charming."

But I soon ceased paying attention to this trick of his I was basking in the sunlight which I noticed was making me feel much better. The sand was beginning to stoke up underfoot and though I was eager for a dip I postponed it for a minute or two more. At last I said to Masson "Shall we go in now" and plunged. Masson walked in gingerly and only began to swim when he was out of his depth. He swam hand over hand and made slow headway, so I left him behind and caught up with Marie. The water was cold and I felt all the better for it. We swam a long way out Marie and I side by side and it was pleasant feeling how our movements matched hers and mine and how we were both in the same mood enjoying every moment.

Albert Camus, *The Stranger*

This is how Albert Camus punctuated his text.

Masson wanted to have a swim at once, but his wife and Raymond were disinclined to move. So only the three of us, Marie, Masson, and myself, went down to the beach. Marie promptly plunged in, but Masson and I waited for a bit. He was rather slow of speech and had, I noticed, a habit of saying "and what's more" between his phrases—even when the second added nothing really to the first. Talking of Marie, he said: "She's an awfully pretty girl, and what's more, charming."

But I soon ceased paying attention to this trick of his; I was basking in the sunlight, which, I noticed, was making me feel much better. The sand was beginning to stoke up underfoot and, though I was eager for a dip, I postponed it for a minute or two more. At last[1] I said to Masson: "Shall we go in now?" and plunged. Masson

1 Keep in mind that a comma is optional for short prepositional phrases.

walked in gingerly and only began to swim when he was out of his depth. He swam hand over hand and made slow headway, so I left him behind and caught up with Marie. The water was cold, and I felt all the better for it. We swam a long way out, Marie and I, side by side, and it was pleasant feeling how our movements matched, hers and mine, and how we were both in the same mood, enjoying every moment.

Albert Camus, *The Stranger*

SIX

USAGE AND COMMON ERRORS

30. SUBJECT / VERB AGREEMENT I

30.1 Subjects and verbs have number. They can be singular or plural. Subjects and verb must agree in number.

- The **dog runs** across the street.
- The **dogs run** across the street.
- The same is true in Latin.
- ***Canis*** *trans viam* ***currit****.*
- ***Canes*** *trans viam* ***currunt****.*

30.2 In the present tense, when the noun is singular, the verb adds an "s." When the noun is plural, the verb does not add an "s."

- The man labors for his uncle.
- The men labor for their uncle.
- The man labored for his uncle.
- The men labored for their uncle.
- The man will labor for his uncle.
- The men will labor for their uncle.

30.3 The following helping verbs also change forms: is/are, was/were, has/have, does/do.

- She is climbing the mountain.
- The women are climbing the mountain
- The teacher was studying.
- The teachers were studying.

- The man has labored for his uncle.
- The men have labored for their uncle.
- Does he care?
- Do they care?

30.4 The following helping verbs do not change forms: can, could, may, might, must should, and will.

- They can go.
- She can go.
- They must go.
- He must go.

30.5 There is / There are. The subject follows the verb.

- There are problems.
- There is a problem.
- Here is the student.
- Here are the students.

30.6 With questions, the verb comes before the subject. Locate the subject to find the correct form of the verb.

- How was the **man** able to get the piano into the door?
- How were the **men** able to get the piano into the door?
- Is the **answer** correct?
- Are the **answers** correct?
- What is the **matter**?
- What are the **matters**?

30.7 The personal pronoun creates a few oddities.

	Singular	Plural
1st	I labor. (Notice the verb is plural.)	We labor.
2nd	You labor. (Notice the verb is plural.)	You labor.
3rd	He labors.	They labor.

30.8 Compound subjects joined with the coordinating conjunction, "and," require a plural verb.

- Jack and Jill run up the hill.
- They run up the hill.
- Jack runs up the hill.

30.9 The coordinating conjunctions, "or" and "nor," follow a different pattern. The number of the verb is determined by the last subject (one closest to the verb). Pay close attention to how the number of the verb changes.

- The boy or the girl **hears** the sound.
- The boys or the girl **hears** the sound.
- The boy or the girls **hear** the sound.
- The boys or the girls **hear** the sound.
- Try this one: The boy, the girl, or the father hear/hears the sound.

EXERCISES:

Choose the correct verb.

1. Do they run / runs businesses effectively in this region?
2. The actor and his friend is / are coming to the party.
3. Her parents or her guardian is / are coming to the conferences.
4. Apple and Amazon is / are two of the most successful companies in the world.
5. The man in the mountainous ranges work / works night and day.
6. There is / are ants in the garden.
7. The soldiers who fought in World War II wear / wears a special badge of honor for their service.
8. The tiger of the most remote jungles prowl / prowls at night and pounce / pounces all types of prey.
9. The lone wolf in the jungles runs/run towards the river.
10. Neither the girls nor the boy care / cares for the dessert on the table.
11. Is / are there a problem?

12. "For in Tashbaan there is / are only one traffic regulation, which is that everyone who is less important has to get out of the way for everyone who is more important..."
    C. S. Lewis, *The Horse and His Boy*

13. He or they has / have to travel by train.

14. Does / Do he or they run / runs the store?

31. SUBJECT / VERB AGREEMENT II

31.1 Some nouns are plural but are singular grammatically.

- News, politics, economics, measles, miles, years, dollars, etc.
- The news reports only good things.
- Politics baffles me.
- Five miles of walking is no joke on a hot day.
- Ten dollars is all I have to my name.

31.2 Collective nouns can be either singular or plural depending on the author's intent, but consistency is necessary. Often it is best to rewrite the sentence when there is any doubt.

- The staff is hungry, and they are deciding what to order.
- The staff is hungry, and it is deciding what to order.
- Better: The staff members are hungry, and they are deciding what to order.

31.3 Don't let prepositional phrases with plural objects confuse you.

- A bouquet of roses and tulips **are** the perfect gift. Incorrect. The subject is "bouquet."
- A bouquet of roses and tulips **is** the perfect gift.
- The pack of hungry wolves looks friendly. To make things clearer, you can just remove the prepositional phrase. The pack ~~of hungry wolves~~ looks friendly.

- It is clearer in Latin: *Manus militum ad urbem ambulat.* The band of soldiers walk to the city.
- The boy, with his friends, is angry. "Along with his parents" is a prepositional phrase.

Exception: "a lot, a majority, some," words that indicate portions. The word that comes after "of" determines the number of the verb.

- A lot of pizza is missing.
- A lot of pizzas are missing.
- Some of the pie is rotten.
- Some of the pies are rotten.
- A quarter of the city is in arms.
- A quarter of the people have armed themselves.
- Most of the juice is gone.
- Most of the juices are gone.

31.4 Like prepositional phrases, relative/adjective clauses can cause confusion. Do not let the intervening clause confuse you. Drawing parentheses will help.

- The athlete (with a host of medals) stands tall.
- The athlete (who has a host of medals) stands tall.
- The athletes (who have won nothing) stand tall.

31.5 The contrary-to-fact (subjunctive), the idea that the situation is not true, follows a different pattern.

- The word "were" in a contrary-to-fact condition is used with a singular subject.
- If the boy were here, he would defend himself.
- If you are in doubt, you can rewrite the sentence: "Were the boy here, he would defend himself."
- I wish it were true.

31.6 The following indefinite pronouns take singular verbs.

Either	Anything	Somebody	No one	One
Neither	Anybody	Everyone	Nothing	
Other	Someone	Everything	Nobody	
Anyone	Something	Everybody	Each	

31.7 The following indefinite pronouns take plural verbs: both, few, many, several, and others.

- Many have tried.
- Both men fail the test.
- Few run for office every year.
- Several hear the call, but only a few respond.
- Notice that the verbs are plural.

31.8 Subject and verb are inverted when the sentence begins with "There is/There are" or "Here is/Here are."

- Here are the books you requested.
- Here is the book you requested.
- There are mice in the laboratory?
- Is there a mouse in the laboratory?

EXERCISES:

Choose the correct verb.

1. Dollars speak / speaks in a world ruled by finances.
2. The media tell / tells the truth most of the time.

3. The thought of the final five miles exert / exerts pressure on marathon runners.
4. The men's strength win / wins the contest.
5. If he was / were present, he would stand up for the truth.
6. Each has / have had a chance to play the game.
7. Several from the committee hear / hears the commotion in the hallways and is / are annoyed.
8. Everyone say / says, "I love you."
9. Does / Do anyone want another slice of peperoni pizza with extra cheese?
10. Every one of the ties has / have a tinge of red, white, and blue.
11. Everybody at the gala was / were having a great time and enjoying the music and company.
12. Someone at the stables clean / cleans the floors.
13. Who is / are the boys who has / have taken the mascot?
14. Either of the guitars is / are for sale.
15. More than anything the staff wish / wishes to take a break.
16. The temperature in the countries of Central Asia is / are unseasonably cold.
17. This wrestler is the one who compete / competes on the national level.
18. There is / are few people who still read and love Sanskrit.
19. Shall everyone in the room leave / leaves the building?

20. If the test was /were easier, I would have passed with flying colors.
21. Some of the pies is / are missing.
22. A lot of the pie is / are eaten.
23. In basic training, nothing is /are easy.
24. The impact of the budget cuts has / have not been felt.

32. PARALLEL CONSTRUCTION

32.1 In lists, consistency is paramount.

- The teacher emphasized clarity, conciseness, and ~~being eloquent~~.
- Notice the being eloquent is a gerund + predicate adjective; the others are nouns.
- The teacher emphasized clarity, conciseness, and eloquence.
- I love to read, to eat, and ~~running~~.
- I love reading, eating, and running.
- I love to read, to eat, and to run.

32.2 Comparisons require consistency.

- I prefer to read a book than ~~watching~~ a documentary.
- I prefer to read a book than to watch a documentary.
- I prefer reading a book than watching a documentary.
- If you start with an infinitive, keep the infinitive construction. If you start with a gerund, keep the gerund construction.

32.3 With linking verbs, both sides must be consistent. A linking verb can be thought of as an equal sign.

- To love is ~~caring.~~
- To love is to care.

- To be or not to be is the question.

32.4 Correlative conjunctions also require parallel construction.

- The runners not only **want the medal** but also **the recognition.** (This construction is not parallel.)
- The runners want not only **the medal** but also **the recognition**.
- The runners not only **want the medal** but also **want the recognition.**

32.5 Longer sentences can also employ parallel construction. Consistency is paramount.

- "Do not the nightly guards placed on the Palatine Hill—do not the watches posted throughout the city—does not the alarm of the people, and the union of all good men—does not the precaution taken of assembling the senate in this most defensible place—do not the looks and countenances of this venerable body here present, have any effect upon you?" Cicero, *Orationes in Catalinam*

- "After this great liberator is laid to rest, and when we have returned to our cities and villages and rejoined our daily routines, let us search for his strength. Let us search for his largeness of spirit somewhere inside of ourselves. And when the night grows dark, when injustice weighs heavy on our hearts, when our best-laid plans seem beyond our reach, let us think of Madiba and the words that brought him comfort within the four walls of his cell..." Barack Obama, On Nelson Mandela, 2013

- "With malice toward none, with charity for all, with firmness in the right as God gives us to see the right, let us strive on to finish the work we are in, to bind up the nation's wounds, to care for him who shall have borne the battle and for his widow and his orphan, to do all which may achieve and cherish a just and lasting peace among ourselves and with all nations." Abraham Lincoln, Second Inaugural Address, 1865.

- "[W]e here highly resolve that these dead shall not have died in vain, that this nation, under God, shall have a new birth of freedom, and that this government of the people, by the people, for the people, shall not perish from the earth." Abraham Lincoln, Gettysburg Address

- These are all examples of tricolons. Reread these examples and study why they work so well.

EXERCISES:

Correct the sentences to ensure the constructions are parallel. If the sentence is correct, leave it alone.

1. The little girl loves to make sandcastles, to eat cookies, and swimming in the sea.
2. I love reading books more than to watch movies.
3. The student is an interesting subject to observe. He shows great academic potential, uncanny curiosity in pop-culture, and is lacking attention in class.

4. My mother said: “To run for office is showing your determination and grit.”
5. His morning routines are reading a chapter of the Bible, singing a song, and to run to school as quickly as possible so that he won’t be late.
6. My father taught me how to cut wood, how to join wood, and painting.
7. While I was waiting in the dentist office, I read a few magazines, watched TV, and was looking at my phone way too much.
8. Not only does he desire the prize but also the accolades.
9. The Spartans fought for their land, for their way of life, and most importantly on account of their freedom.
10. The intern was responsible for copying, editing, and the all-important lunch order.
11. Is it really a greater joy to give than receiving?
12. Running a company can result is great success or its opposite, experiencing great failure.
13. The spies planned to sneak into the archives at night to steal the sensitive data, to snoop around, and for the purpose of planning their next attack.
14. She is honest, capable, and works diligently.
15. People go to New York for rest, relaxation, and to go shopping.

16. My friend took me to see a movie and golfing.
17. My mother not only likes to make tea but also drink it.
18. When I came home from a long trip, I settled into my routines—work, play, and resting.
19. I would rather eat a sandwich than eating a salad.
20. The senator is not only swayed by his appetites but also special interest groups.

COMPOSITION:

1. Write a sentence with a tricolon (with parallel construction).

____

____

____

____

____

2. Write a sentence with parallel construction that uses three infinitive phrases.

____

____

3. Write a sentence with parallel construction that uses three gerund phrases.

33. HYPERCORRECTIONS

33.1 Hypercorrections take place when a student imperfectly understands a rule and overextends its usage.

33.2 Subject and object confusion can take place when people use the predicate nominative incorrectly.

- My friend and I hailed a taxi in the pouring rain. ("My friend" and "I" are the subjects. So, the usage of "I" is correct.)
- The taxi picked up my friend and me in the pouring rain. (This sentence is correct as well because "me" is the direct object.)
- The taxi picked up my friend and I in the pouring rain. (An example of hypercorrection. We need a direct object, and "me" is the correct direct object.)
- Is this sentence correct? Give him and I a second chance.
- Between you and I. "Between" is a preposition. So, it should be: "between you and me."

33.3 Do not use a reflexive when a simple pronoun will do.

- He is going to the party with Josh and myself.
- He is going to the party with John and me.
- Josh and myself will be there.
- Josh and I will be there.

33.4 "Whom" and "Whomever" are often used incorrectly.

- Whomever told you it was correct is mistaken.
- It should be: Whoever told you it was correct is mistaken.

33.5 Don't replace adjectives with adverbs.

- "I feel terribly." It should be "I feel terrible."
- "This seems excellent" is correct, so is "She died young."
- The adjectives are all complements to the verb.

33.6 Not all words that end in "us" or "um" come from Latin.

- The plural of octopus is octopuses, not octopi.
- When in doubt, look up the word.

EXERCISES:

Correct the hypercorrections. If there is no error, leave the sentence alone.

1. I can't wait for Shakespeare in the Park over the summer. John and myself will be there.
2. The manager gave the assignment to you and I. Let's do a great job.
3. The pandemic showed us that different kinds of viri can spread at alarming rates, especially with the ease of travel.

4. The hotel arranged an early morning pick up to take my parents and I to the airport.
5. Whom will volunteer for the task?
6. Now that we are entering into election season, all eyes will be on the Iowa cauci.
7. The coach yelled: "Hurry and pass the ball to whomever is open."
8. Between you and I, the solution to the math problem can only be solved by making a bar diagram.
9. When the teacher looks at Martha and me, I feel anxious even though we are innocent.
10. After the incident concerning the rats, pigeons, and bugs, the boys feel terribly.
11. The trainer looked at the boxer and said: "Don't worry. The story about you and I will be told in due time."
12. The moral critic shouted, "The problem with people today is that they only care about their stati. Only appearances matter."

34. IRREGULAR PLURALS AND MISUSED WORDS

34.1 Some nouns have irregular plurals. Here is a partial list.

Singular	Plural
Addendum	Addenda
Alumna	Alumnae
Alumnus	Alumni
Appendix	Appendices
Cherub	Cherubim
Deer	Deer
Die	Dice
Elf	Elves
Knife	Knives
Loaf	Loaves
Mouse	Mice
Ox	Oxen
Swine	Swine
Thesis	Theses

34.2 These words are often misused. It is worth memorizing this list.

Accept means to receive. Except means to omit.	I accept the position. Except dairy, I can eat anything.
Advert means to turn the mind or attention. Avert means to ward off something.	He adverted to an earlier point. Exercising can avert heart disease.
Advice means council; it is a noun. Advise means to give council; it is a verb.	Solomon needed advice. The elders advised Solomon.
Affect means to influence. Effect means to accomplish.	Her eloquence affected the panel. Her eloquence effected lasting change.
Aggravate means to make worse not to irritate.	The insult will aggravate the bad situation.
Allusion means a reference. Illusion is a misleading image.	The allusion to Homer was vague but real. The levitation was an illusion of mirrors.

Appraise means to estimate. Apprise means to inform.	He appraised the house above market value. He will apprise us when the markets rise.
Beside means at the side of someone or something. Besides means "in addition to."	He swam beside the dolphins. She is the best swimmer on the team. Besides, she is our valedictorian.
Can means able. May denotes permission.	The dog can climb the stairs. May I go to the bathroom?
Cliché is a noun, not an adjective.	Avoid clichés. It would be wrong to say: "That is so cliché."
Complement means to complete. Compliment is a word of admiration.	To complement his outfit, Tim needs a bowtie. Tim received many compliments on his bowtie.
Credible means believable. Credulous means gullible.	The nun was a credible witness. The credulous boy believed everything.

Disinterested means impartial. Uninterested means bored.	The disinterested jury was perfect. I can't blame the boy for being uninterested in quantum physics.
Elicit means to draw out. Illicit means illegal.	The officer elicited facts by being kind. The illicit material was in his bag.
Emigrate means to leave a home country. Immigrate means to move into a new country.	He emigrated from the old land and immigrated to New York City.
Enervate means to weaken, not to energize.	The workout enervated the old man.
Fulsome means excessively insincere. The connotation is negative. It does not mean full.	The sincere CEO offered a fulsome apology for lying to the public. (Incorrect usage) The people did not believe in the fulsome apology of the CEO who drove off in his red Ferrari. (Correct usage)
Flaunt means to show off. Flout means to treat with contempt.	Many celebrities flaunt their wealth and flout rules.

Hone means to sharpen or to refine. Home (as a verb) pertains to the ability of animals to return to its original territory.	The boy honed his skills of training homing pigeons.
Insure pertains to insurance. Ensure means to make sure that something happens.	Geico insured me. I ensured my mother that I have insurance.
Ingenious means extraordinary creativity. Ingenuous means childlike simplicity.	The solution to the math problem was ingenious. The child was innocent and ingenuous.
Meretricious mean offensively insincere. Meritorious means full of merits.	The meretricious look of the avaricious broker sent warning signals to investors. The good deeds were meritorious.
Principal means main (as an adjective). Principle means basic tenet or law.	The principal ingredients are salt and garlic. The principle of the document is equality.

Proscribe means to condemn and forbid. Prescribe means to recommend, as in doctors prescribe.	The dictator proscribed the freedom of speech. The doctor prescribes long walks to lower stress.
Simplistic means naïvely simple. Simple means simple in the best sense.	You want a simple course of action, not a simplistic one.
Than is a conjunction in a comparison. Then is an adverb that refers to time.	Sam is taller than Jane. Then I will come.

EXERCISES:

Choose any pair of commonly misused words and write one sentence that incorporates both meanings correctly.

1. The solution of the child prodigy was incredibly simple, not simplistic—all superfluous points were cut out and got to the heart of the issue.

2. ____

____

____

____

____

____

____

____

____

3. ____

____

____

____

____

____

____

4. ____

____

____

____

____

____

____

____

5. ____

____

____

____

____

____

____

____

6. ____

____

____

____

____

____

____

____

7. ____

____

____

____

____

____

____

____

8. ____

____

____

____

____

____

____

____

9. ____

____

____

____

____

____

____

____

10. ____

35. ODDS AND ENDS

35.1 In titles, the first letter is capitalized except articles, prepositions, and conjunctions of fewer than four letters.

- *The Chronicles of Narnia.*
- *The Hobbit*
- *Of Mice and Men*
- *To Kill a Mockingbird*
- Movies, long poems, full-length plays, magazines, and journals are also italicized.

35.2 Poems, articles, and short works receive quotation marks.

- Arthur Darby Nock's article, "Religious Attitudes of the Ancient Greeks," is very insightful.
- I love Seamus Heaney's poem, "Scaffolding."

35.3 Coordinating and non-coordinating adjectives.

- If you can put the conjunction "and" between the adjectives, then the adjectives are coordinating and receive a comma.
- He is a nice, kind, thoughtful boy.
- If you cannot put the conjunction "and," then the adjectives are non-coordinating and do not receive a comma.
- I have a silver German mechanical pencil.

35.4 Dashes

- A dash can introduce an appositive. See §14.
- "I read three books in the last month—*To Kill a Mockingbird, The Confessions of St. Augustine,* and *The Meditations.*"
- Dashes also create pauses. "The students, faculty, and parents—are all to praise for a great year."

36. PUTTING IT ALL TOGETHER

I. Punctuate. All punctuation has been removed except for periods and question marks.

"I heard a light sigh and then my heart stood still stopped dead short by an exulting and terrible cry by the cry of inconceivable triumph and of unspeakable pain. 'I knew it—I was sure!'... She knew. She was sure. I heard her weeping she had hidden her face in her hands. It seemed to me that the house would collapse before I could escape that the heavens would fall upon my head. But nothing happened. The heavens do not fall for such a trifle. Would they have fallen, I wonder if I had rendered Kurtz that justice which was his due? Hadnt he said he wanted only justice? But I couldn't. I could not tell her. It would have been too dark—too dark altogether..." "Marlow ceased, and sat apart indistinct and silent in the pose of a meditating Buddha. Nobody moved for a time. "We have lost the first of the ebb," said the Director suddenly. I raised my head. The offing was barred by a black bank of clouds and the tranquil waterway leading to the uttermost ends of the earth flowed sombre under an overcast sky—seemed to lead into the heart of an immense darkness."

This is how Joseph Conrad punctuated his text. Notice the stylistic flexibility.

"I heard a light sigh and then my heart stood still, stopped dead short by an exulting and terrible cry, by the cry of inconceivable triumph and of unspeakable pain. 'I knew it—I was sure!'... She knew. She was sure. I heard her weeping; she had hidden her face in her hands. It seemed to me that the house would collapse before I could escape, that the heavens would fall upon my head. But nothing happened. The heavens do not fall for such a trifle. Would they have fallen, I wonder, if I had rendered Kurtz that justice which was his due? Hadn't he said he wanted only justice? But I couldn't. I could not tell her. It would have been too dark—too dark altogether..."

"Marlow ceased, and sat apart, indistinct and silent, in the pose of a meditating Buddha. Nobody moved for a time. "We have lost the first of the ebb," said the Director suddenly. I raised my head. The offing was barred by a black bank of clouds, and the tranquil waterway leading to the uttermost ends of the earth flowed sombre under an overcast sky—seemed to lead into the heart of an immense darkness."

Joseph Conrad, *Heart of Darkness*

II. Identity the underlined words, drawing arrows where appropriate.

"It goes a long way back, some twenty years. All my life I had been looking for something, and everywhere I turned someone tried to tell me **what it was**. I accepted their answers too, **though they were often in contradiction and even self-contradictory**. I was naïve. I was looking for myself and asking everyone except myself questions **which I, and only I, could answer**. It took me a long time and much painful boomeranging of my expectations **to achieve a realization everyone else appears to have been born with**: That I am nobody but myself. But first I had to discover **that I am an invisible man!**

And yet I am no freak of nature, nor of history. I was in the cards, **other things having been equal (or unequal) eighty-five years ago**. I am not ashamed of my grandparents for having been slaves. I am only ashamed of myself **for having at one time been ashamed**. About eighty-five years ago they were told that they were free, united with others of our country in everything pertaining to the common good, and, in everything social, separate like the fingers of the hand. And they believed it. They exulted in it. They stayed in their place, worked hard, and brought up my father to do the same. But my grandfather is the **one**. He was an odd old guy, my grandfather, and I am told **I take after him**. It was he who caused the trouble. On his deathbed he called my father to him and said, 'Son, after I'm gone I want you to keep up the good fight. I **never** told you, but our life is a war and I have been a traitor all my born days, a spy in the enemy's country ever since I give up my gun back in the Reconstruction. Live **with your head** in the lion's mouth. I want you to overcome 'em with yeses, undermine 'em with grins, agree 'em to death and destruction, let 'em swoller you till they vomit or bust wide open.' They thought **the old man had gone out of his mind.** He had been the meekest of men. The younger children were rushed from the room, the shades **drawn** and the flame of the lamp turned so low that it sputtered on the wick like the old man's breathing. 'Learn it to the younguns,' he whispered fiercely; then he died."

Ralph Ellison, *Invisible Man*

III. Draw parentheses around all dependent clauses, drawing arrows where appropriate.

1. "Now, what is the difference between the two? How does one determine when a law is just or unjust? A just law is a man-made code that squares with the moral law, or the law of God. An unjust law is a code that is out of harmony with the moral law. To put it in the terms of St. Thomas Aquinas, an unjust law is a human law that is not rooted in eternal and natural law. Any law that uplifts human personality is just. Any law that degrades human personality is unjust. All segregation statutes are unjust because segregation distorts

the soul and damages the personality." Martin Luther King, "Letter from a Birmingham Jail"

2. "I have already, on a previous occasion, spoken at some length on the subject of Work and Vocation. What I urged then was a thoroughgoing revolution in our whole attitude to work. I asked that it should be looked upon, not as a necessary drudgery to be undergone for the purpose of making money, but as a way of life in which the nature of man should find its proper exercise and delight and so fulfill itself to the glory of God. That it should, in fact, be thought of as a creative activity undertaken for the love of the work itself; and that man, made in God's image, should make things, as God makes them, for the sake of doing well a thing that is well worth doing." Dorothy Sayers, "Why Work?"

IV. Underline all verbals and label.

1. Watching the foreign film made me realize that I need to learn more about different cultures.
2. The young girl carried the bruised book wherever she went; it must be the book to read.
3. Running to catch the train, Mr. Jones dropped his phone down the sewer.

4. He stepped down, trying not to look long at her, as if she were the sun, yet he saw her, like the sun, even without looking. Leo Tolstoy, *Anna Karenina*

5. Who, being loved, is poor? Oscar Wilde

V. Write a short paragraph on the most meaningful piece of advice someone gave to you. This paragraph should include: three verbals, parallel construction, at least one compound/complex sentence, and punctuation should be perfect. Be prepared to share your paragraph with your classmates.

____

____

____

____

____

____

____

____

____

____

____

Congratulations are in order. You now have greater knowledge to compose sturdy and varied prose. You also can begin developing your distinct voice. A lifetime of putting together words awaits you. Enough said. Well done.

THE END!

ABOUT THE AUTHOR

John Lee is an educator who seeks to inspire students to achieve excellence in their studies and their lives. He has taught at St. Thomas Choir School, Drew University, Nyack College, St. Bernard's School, and The Geneva School of Manhattan. He obtained his M.A., M.Phil. and Ph.D. in history from Yale University. His essays have appeared in *The Banner, Mere Orthodoxy, Christianity Today,* and a number of other outlets. He lives in New York City and East Hampton with his wife and two children.